THE CAREGIVER PRINCIPLES™

A Step-By-Step Process that Meets You Where You Are on the Caregiver Journey, Helping You Build Your Own Roadmap Forward to Power Through This Season with Greater Resiliency, Perspective, Gratitude, and Renewal

MICHAEL A. BOYLAN

—OTHER BOOKS BY THE AUTHOR—

The Power To Get In
TEETH: Does Your Value Position Have Any?
Accelerants
Reach For Me: The Story of My Son Connor
The Power To Get Justice
The Caregiver Principles (the first in a series of four books)

THE
CAREGIVER
PRINCIPLES™

A Step-By-Step Process that Meets You Where You Are on the Caregiver Journey, Helping You Build Your Own Roadmap Forward to Power Through This Season with Greater Resiliency, Perspective, Gratitude, and Renewal

BY MICHAEL A. BOYLAN

"Caregiving is universal. There are only four kinds of people in the world: those who have been caregivers, those who currently are caregivers, those who will be caregivers, and those who will need caregivers."

—Rosalynn Carter, former First Lady of The United States of America

PUBLISHED BY LEVEL PRESS — MINNEAPOLIS, MINNESOTA

NOTICE OF INTELLECTUAL PROPERTY & TRADEMARK PROTECTION

First published in the United States of America.
Official Publication Date: October 15, 2026
Copyright © 2026 by Michael A. Boylan. All rights reserved.
Library of Congress Catalog-in-Publications Data.
Cover design and layout by Megan French Design, Phoenix, Arizona.
Print production by P.H. Lanpher Consulting of Minneapolis, Minnesota.
Printed by Corporate Graphics, Minneapolis, Minnesota.
ISBN Number: 979-8-9943703-0-8
First Edition, Hard Cover, Printed in the United States of America

Praise for this Book

Praise for this Book

Praise for this Book

Praise for this Book

TABLE OF CONTENTS

FOREWORD

In the positioning and architecting of one of the most successful best-selling books of all time, *The Seven Habits of Highly Effective People* (twenty-five million copies sold), and corporate training program based upon the book that has been adopted by more than 400 of the Fortune 500 organizations around the world, I was fortunate to be directly involved in the shaping of the material and step-by-step process that has not only been successful and well regarded, but even more importantly, has impacted the lives of millions of good people in helping them lead more productive, meaningful, and rewarding lives.

This is why I am honored to be involved with the material that you are about to be introduced to, and the step-by-step process outlined in this book. This material could be as impactful in improving your life, your well-being, your outlook, and your resiliency, as any material I have ever been associated with.

I would ask that you come to this book with an open mind and an open heart as to where the process could lead you in terms of improving your life.

The principles, the process, and the exercises offered throughout the book are designed to help you shape your own roadmap forward by addressing the issues, challenges, and hardships that you are experiencing, which can be very challenging. And other times, they offer life lessons with the understanding that each caregiver's journey is unique.

With the many articles, studies, and research about the challenges that caregivers (what the research says are over seventy-five million adults in the U.S. alone, meaning 25% of the adult population) face emotionally, physically, financially, and spiritually, this topic is very close to many. And yet caregivers are the first ones to tell you that they take care of their loved ones **first** and themselves (usually) **last**.

This (as you already know) is not helpful to you. I am not telling you anything you have not already heard before. Therefore, take this book, the process it outlines, and the exercises offered you as your opportunity to build a better life for yourself and your family, in the middle of all the chaos that may be going on around you.

Caring for the Caregiver is a foundational principle that underscores this material. Material with the ability to help you chart a new course to power through with a new mindset, a sense of gratitude, and resiliency that lifts up your own well-being as you move forward.

And we begin by honoring and recognizing your commitment to the loved ones you are caring for!

—Bob Thele, former President/Chief Executive Officer,
The Covey Leadership Center (now Franklin-Covey),
Architect behind the success of The Seven Habits of Highly Effective People, *international bestselling book and corporate training program adopted by over 400 of Fortune 500 companies worldwide*

THE CAREGIVER MANTRA

I am a caregiver.
I am a proud caregiver.
And I pledge that I will do my very best,
to provide good and compassionate care for my loved one.
With understanding, with empathy, and respect.
Regardless of the hills and valleys present in my own life,
or that may be ahead.
I ask for grace, for patience and perspective along this journey,
which could last a while.
And for the wisdom to make good decisions for myself, my family,
and for my loved one along the journey.

I am a proud caregiver.

A MESSAGE FROM THE LEADERSHIP TEAM OF REACH FOR ME

We want to welcome you to a group of people who live in the world of caregiving. We understand the journey and have the utmost respect, compassion, and concern for you and for your well-being in whatever season of the journey you may be in right now.

As you know, the role of a caregiver often has no end in sight. It requires the constant giving of yourself, while keeping all other aspects of your life spinning/moving forward at the same time, which is not an easy task. The constant giving of yourself can feel as though your own individual needs are no longer important, because you are a caregiver.

Some say there is no greater calling in life than to be in this role. It may not be a role you choose, or one you planned for, and yet it requires your all. There are many stages and ranges of emotions that you go through when this role becomes part of your world. The **Personal Caregiver Roadmap** can be an invaluable tool for you as you encounter the challenges that will surely come your way.

What is important for you to know is that in Reach For Me, you have a partner that has been there, is there, and has gone before you to provide wisdom, strength, and the courage to navigate these unchartered times. You are not alone. You are loved and appreciated for who you are, and we recognize the difficulties of your own unique journey.

Reach For Me can advocate for the issues and situations you will most likely encounter along the way, helping you maintain your sanity. We are your partner on this road.

This is why we have organized a system for you; a step-by-step process that will be of tremendous value as a guiding light to help you find your way along your own path. Many times, a caregiver's path seems to have no end in sight. In those times, we all need a helping hand. Your Personal Caregiver Roadmap. Your plan for how you will navigate the challenges on your plate and power through them to the best of your abilities. It can truly be a lifesaver for you.

With Reach For Me, that helping hand comes from those who have travelled that road (and still are) and have a desire to be there for you because they recognize the compassion and care that you will require along the way, so you can power through with greater resiliency, self-awareness, self-care, and gratitude. Caring for the Caregiver. Our mission.

Welcome to the family of Reach For Me.

BASELINE LEVEL-SET: SOME PERSPECTIVE AND WHY IT'S RELEVANT

A little dose of perspective as we begin together. We are all well-aware that we come into this world needing lots of help. And we leave this world in much the same way, needing help from others, in many cases. It's the circle of life, shall we say. It's the part of life in the middle, when we become self-sufficient and don't need to depend on anyone else to get along that actually makes caregiving challenging. Why? Because we go about our work and our life as we desire, unless some tragedy or situation keeps us from pursuing the life that we want. This middle part of life is, in some respects, why caregiving is considered such a radical pattern interrupt because we've been able to lead our lives (pretty much) exactly as we want.

This period of self-sufficiency is what can cause our life as a caregiver to be challenging, even difficult, based upon how independent we've been able to be over the years.

When we are called upon to assist or take care of someone else, regardless of who it is, that throws us a curveball because it interrupts our life, our plans, our work, professional pursuits, career goals, vacations, and our family time. And that is when life can get more stressful, complicated, and downright challenging. Those in the caregiving boat right now understand what I'm talking about because they are living these things week after week.

Like the quote from the former First Lady of the United States says, the world of caregiving will likely touch your life at some point. And when it does, those who do not adjust well, or are not willing to adjust their lives to provide the care, focused attention, emotional bandwidth, and the time to someone else, will struggle. Caregiving for some extended period of time is not only hard, but it can (and does) take a toll on you mentally, emotionally, physically, financially, and spiritually! It touches **all** areas of your life.

As the single father of an adult special-needs son, I have been raising and caring for my son for more than twenty years totally on my own. I understand what it can be like, and how it is easy to lose yourself in the process of caring for another person, regardless of whether they are an underage or adult special-needs child, an aging parent, a spouse or significant other, a military veteran, or another disabled loved one.

As the oldest of five siblings with an aging eighty-six-year-old mother, I was also involved in providing care for her right up and until the time of her passing from a brain tumor. I was directly involved with all that that entailed, from coordinating with the doctors, hospitals, oncologists, brain surgeon, and hospice care teams, to dealing with health insurance, the long-term care insurance corporation, hospice-care facility, and keeping an eye on the care teams in both the hospital and hospice-care facilities. As you may know, these places are often owned and operated by large entities who are primarily focused on the bottom line, versus making sure they have proper levels of staffing (which they often don't). Of course, their talking tracks are different. However, pay close attention to how thinly staffed many of these facilities are and you'll understand what I'm referring to. You must keep a close eye on these facilities to make sure you are getting the care for your loved one that you are paying for.

It's amazing (and frustrating) how much effort is often required (in addition to caring for your loved one), to make certain their professional medical and care staff are providing the care and services you are already paying for! That alone, is a job in and of itself.

All the factors that converge on us caregivers all at once throw us into a new world, putting us into a state where there are different balls in the air all at the same time, which is why it can be challenging to keep your head above water.

Add to this the new emotions, the anger, confusion, the doubts, the feelings of loneliness and exhaustion that can overtake us without much warning, impacting our relationships, the family dynamic, and our working life.

This is why caregiving can cause plenty of disruption in your life. And why it is paramount that you take this **new season** seriously, by equipping yourself and your family with a living guide—a **toolset** you can use to power through to the best of your abilities, improving your resiliency and emotional well-being as you provide care for a loved one for some extended period.

That is the value of what this book can do for you. It can serve as a living, breathing, active toolset—a step-by-step process that can be of immense help to you, your siblings, and your family, as you get drawn into what may be a new world. Hopefully, this new world goes as smoothly as possible, though I must prepare you.

The life of caregiving can dredge up some very intense challenges—all of which you will have to confront at some point. However, the good thing about this life of caregiving, whether you've been at it for a while or are brand new to it, is it also gives us opportunities to be grateful, have some perspective, and give back to the person who is now in need of your time, your care, patience, and understanding. Things that were more than likely given to you without any strings attached!

Whether you are caring for an underage or adult special-needs child, an aging parent, a spouse, a military veteran, or another loved one, the power of the process in this book will help you to better assess and deal with the host of matters that will come into your world (if they haven't already). Challenges that will pull at your heart, your mind, your money, your physical abilities, your beliefs, as well as your faith.

When this happens, you can use this process to build your plan to power through with more patience, empathy, and resiliency. Your Personal Caregiver Roadmap will help you better navigate and endure whatever lies ahead on this road of unknowns.

The **Personal Caregiver Roadmap** is a custom-designed guide and approach plan created by you, the caregiver. It is a roadmap that you will use to **address** and **navigate** the added challenges thrust upon all caregivers and families, helping power through the emotional, physical, financial, and spiritual challenges that are part of the journey. It will help protect your mental health, well-being, and resiliency. And you can update your plan at any time.

As you already know, caregiving requires a tremendous out-pouring of yourself on many different levels, requiring new levels of patience and endurance that (perhaps) has not been part of your everyday life.

So, the question to ponder as we go through the pages in this book and you begin to build your roadmap forward is, how are you going to show up for the person who now needs some of your time, attention, money, patience, and love? It's a question worthy of reflection as we move through this book together.

Let's begin.

INTRODUCTION
HIGH-LEVEL OVERVIEW AND OUTLINE OF THE BOOK

Welcome to the family of caregivers and thank you for picking up this book! A book that can truly be life-changing for you and for your family, helping you better assess all that is on your plate and navigate through this season with more hope, strength, resiliency, and a newfound perspective toward the one you are caring for.

If you find yourself exhausted, worried, or filled with doubt about what may lie ahead for you and for the loved one you are caring for, welcome. This book and the process it outlines can help you.

If you are sad beyond words after receiving news that your loved one has been diagnosed with dementia, this book will support and help you navigate all of the uncertainties ahead.

If you find yourself angry, frustrated, or stunned by the lack of support from other siblings regarding caring for your loved one, welcome. This book can absolutely help you.

If you feel as though you have lost your identity and are consumed with figuring out how to manage your caregiver responsibilities with everything else on your plate, welcome. This book will help you power through.

If you have received a diagnosis regarding your special-needs child, mom or dad, your spouse or significant other, or another family member who is disabled and are struggling to make sense of it all, this process will help you.

If you are battling with a medical institution or provider, government entity, healthcare insurance company, doctor's office, or the Veterans Affairs (VA) over care your loved one needs, but are being ignored at every turn, exhausting you as you go about advocating for what's best for your loved one, welcome. The process can help you.

If you are scared about what the future holds for you, your family, and your special-needs child, this book will bring you comfort.

If you have been caring for a military veteran and wonder how much longer you can hold up, knowing that they put their life on the line for their country, welcome. The process this book outlines will help you.

If you are concerned about hanging on to your job while keeping up with your caregiver responsibilities, this book can help you.

If you are feeling totally alone, fried, and just not yourself anymore, and are pondering what impact your caregiving demands will have on the relationship with your partner, girlfriend or boyfriend, siblings, and your family, welcome. This book will help you a great deal.

If you are worried about how things will play out given your caregiver responsibilities, wanting to be there for your loved one so that you have no feelings of guilt, this book will help you.

And if you feel there's the potential that this season could change or damage your relationships with other siblings, or with one or both parents, welcome. The roadmap you will build can and will help you.

As we all know, no two caregivers have the same experience, the same caregiver challenges and responsibilities to deal with, or the same financial challenges that caregiving forces upon us. Most of us will have to address how this season will impact our finances, because it will.

My hope is that this book not only provides some perspective in the heat of your responsibilities, but that the process will be of tremendous help in giving you the courage, the wisdom, and resiliency to power through your caregiver responsibilities. The tools within will support you in the most intense of times.

Because we are pulled in different directions, I thought it would be helpful if I provided an overview about how the material is organized with the goal of providing solid benefit for you and others involved in the care of your loved one. Therefore, here is a high-level overview of the material and why it could be a lifesaver for you and any others involved in the caregiving with you.

As the subtitle on the cover states, this book lays out a **step-by-step process—a methodology**—a set of **guidelines** designed to meet you where you are as a caregiver, helping you to power through what has been, is now, or may be challenging times that you are dealing with, or that you see coming around the corner. That's part of the challenge. It's difficult to know what is ahead—forcing you to be flexible. Something most of us are not good at. This creates anxiety, given it is almost impossible to know how long this season of caregiving will last.

Chapter One provides a background as to how I came to this life. As a single father of an adult son diagnosed with Williams syndrome on the autism spectrum by Children's Hospital Minneapolis and confirmed by The University of Minnesota Hospital, I have raised my son all on my own for the last twenty years, with all the hills and valleys associated with this journey. My caregiver responsibilities may continue until I pass away. I don't really know at this point.

Caring for my son has forced a reordering of my professional life, my priorities, my thoughts about what's important and what is not, and other things that caregiving forces upon you—whether you welcome them or not.

As the oldest of five siblings, I was also directly involved with the care of my aging mother and her sudden health challenges after she was diagnosed with a stage 4 brain tumor (glioblastoma). The cancer took her life in a short period, leaving us with emotional loose ends given the speed of her decline, which none of us were prepared for.

Based on two decades of experience as a sole caregiver to my special-needs adult son, I understand the intensity of it all in terms of how caregiving impacts you mentally, emotionally, physically, financially, and spiritually. It can challenge us in all these areas.

It was not long after I had delivered a two-hour keynote address to six thousand attendees at the Microsoft Annual Global Partners Conference that I learned of my son's official diagnosis. I knew then that one day, I would build a process and a program to help caregivers of loved ones to power through with empathy, more perspective, resiliency, and gratitude. Especially in the tough patches, when it feels like the wheels to your life are coming off and you're being pushed to your absolute limit!

Caregiving can be lonely, hard, and taxing on your mind and on your body, impacting other areas of your life, like your work, your relationships, and even your desire to do something for yourself. Couple this with the brutal reality that we live in a culture where most people prefer to focus on the positive; things that are happy, fun, light-hearted and not so damn heavy! However—who can be positive all the time when your emotional, physical, financial, and spiritual resources are under constant pressure?

This is why caregivers will self-isolate to find respite. It is easy to feel as though we are not welcome in our family, or group of friends. Because unless they are living the caregiver experience, it's common to feel somewhat shunned in your circles, because they can't (or won't) support you in your walk. They're happy to give you advice. But they often are not that interested in listening. I have found this to be true in my own experience with my son. Therefore, don't be surprised if you experience this in your walk.

I do not mean this as a downer, but rather as an honest disclosure. I have experienced intense stress worrying about how I was going to handle my caregiving responsibilities, and the lack of interest from others in not wanting to hear about how tough things might be. It can make oneself depressed when you experience how little others care to lend a hand.

In ultra-challenging times, I have put off doctor's appointments for myself because I didn't have the energy or the time to schedule the appointments. I know that this is stupid! However, I bring this up because I understand how a primary caregiver can get overwhelmed and run-down, which not only hurts the caregiver, but the person they are caring for. Suffice it to say, I live it. Another reason why I wrote this book, because of how much it will help you.

Chapter Two provides some mind-blowing data regarding the scope of how many people are on a similar journey. Research states there are an estimated seventy-five million people providing a minimum of twenty hours per week (unpaid) of care to a loved one. That's almost 25% of the adult population.

This is why Rosalynn Carter's quote about caregivers is so relevant. Chapter Two provides more about the scope of the issue and why it is important for us to band together into one network that is exclusive to us. There's power in numbers. Connection allows us to uplift one another through our shared experiences and save money as we grow in influence. More on this later in the book.

Chapter Three shares how it is often impossible to plan for being a caregiver. Often there is no preparation, as the role can come upon us by an accident, an emergency, an out-of-the-blue health challenge, or some combination of the above. And because most of us don't care much for surprises (unless it's a nice gift), caregiving often hands us what many call a "pattern interrupt" in our lives. It forces us to reorder or reprioritize certain things, which causes the stress, anxiety, and uncertainty. All things we don't much care for.

To this very point, there's an exercise coming shortly that I encourage you to complete and share with those in your circle called The Caregiver Preparation Assessment. It will help you begin to think through what issues you may encounter when you get drawn into the world of caregiving.

As shared, this transition is often a trial-by-fire type situation, where a different life is thrust upon us, which we're supposed to just magically adjust to, without making any fuss! Is that realistic? HELL NO! Most people are quite accomplished at making a fuss, in addition to letting others know that we are being inconvenienced by this or that change in our lives. However, this new life will likely press up against and challenge you if it hasn't already.

Your mental strength, your resiliency, your mindset, your faith life, your finances, your personal and work-related relationships, and your family dynamics will likely all be impacted in some manner. Nothing is off the table. Why do things get so intense? Because someone you love and care deeply about needs your help, sometimes forcing you to reprioritize things that are important in your life.

Chapter Four is designed to prepare you for things that could literally blindside you. Relationships you have built with your spouse or life partner, siblings, extended family, friends, even your coworkers, could be tested depending upon the specifics of your situation as a caregiver.

People you thought would support you or help out from time to time, won't. They may even turn their back on you for reasons that they feel are justified. Hence, not only will you need to be resilient as you provide care, but it will require perseverance (and forgiveness) as you experience people who are close to you, who elect not to help out, or worse, turn on you, with the attitude that your journey is not really as difficult as you may be saying it is. These are some of the reasons why it can feel as though the fabric of your life is being uprooted, which is the last thing you need when you are being called to give more of yourself to someone else in need.

Chapter Five gives you the awesome opportunity to peer into the lives of two different families and their caregiver challenges, providing you the chance (at the end of each story) to act as that family's therapist. You will be asked to provide advice as to what that family ought to do to power through the challenges they are dealing with. Both stories represent real-life situations central to millions of caregivers in this country and across the world. You will find both stories to be helpful for building your Personal Caregiver Roadmap.

Chapter Six begins to outline the heart of the book: The Caregiver Principles. This is the name of the step-by-step process that you will use to assess the challenges and dynamics of your situation so that you can begin to build your own Personal Caregiver Roadmap forward.

There are seven principles in total designed to fit together hand-inglove to help you create your roadmap. A process designed to support you regardless of where you are on the journey! A guide to powering through and maintaining your health and resiliency, which is paramount.

Each principle provides the opportunity to think through and assess key elements of your caregiver journey, so you can make decisions around what you need to do to power through with empathy, resiliency, and even some gratitude.

Chapter Seven is where you will bring it all together. You will use the decisions you've made as you went through each of the seven principles (called your *work product*) and incorporate them into one approach plan: your Personal Caregiver Roadmap for how you will move forward.

Chapter Eight provides suggestions to keep your roadmap current and relevant as you encounter new challenges you weren't expecting, or that have caused a change to your life and that of your loved one—which you'll need to compensate for as your journey unfolds.

It is impossible to predict or forecast how your journey will unfold. You'll have your roadmap for how you plan to move forward, but remaining flexible is key so that you don't lose your mind. Just as any organization goes about updating its plans, it's go-to-markets strategy, financial forecasts, budgets, and the like, so, too, will it be necessary to keep your roadmap up-to-date like any organization, so that it addresses the current state of your situation.

This roadmap is your plan for how you feel you should proceed forward based upon the specifics of your journey.

Chapter Nine shares different ways to attain ongoing support with other caregivers in your employer organization, so you are supported at work, in your community, your place of worship, etc.

Getting into a weekly caregiver support group meetup with other caregivers will also help! Hearing other caregivers' challenges and what they are dealing with provides perspective, and the comfort of knowing that you are not alone. Joining a weekly caregiver support group meetup is one way we can all care for the caregiver.

In summary, this book and the step-by-step process it outlines is vital for your mental health and resiliency, and for that of your family. It provides a methodology to assess your current caregiver situation so you can better **address** and **navigate** all that may come at you in this season, protecting your emotional well-being, enriching your caregiver experience, and giving you a better life all at the same time. That is the true power of what this book can do for you.

As one (full-time) caregiver to another, I live this life and am very familiar with the highs and the lows, the emotional swings this life can bring, the doubt, the confusion, and the exhaustion you may be feeling right now. Not to mention the uncertainty around what might be ahead. This road can be brutal. It can take everything out of you and come back for more. This is why I applaud your courage to do your best for your loved one, while taking care of yourself. This is so important.

Because of the intensity and the nature of the journey, I have done my best to shape this book and material in such a way that it not only helps you survive along the various points of the journey, but that the tools, suggestions, and the plan you will build will empower you to improve your life and the life of the one you are caring for. This has been my guiding light as I have created this book for you.

Lastly, my hope is this book will bring us closer as a people, so we are more empathetic and compassionate toward those in need of our help, and our time. I hope it will help buoy ourselves as we provide care to someone else, while protecting our mental, emotional, physical, financial, and spiritual health at the same time. And that our experience deepens our appreciation for those who have helped us along the way.

Let's keep moving forward.

CAREGIVERS' REFLECTIONS (IN THEIR OWN WORDS)

In preparation for this book, I've spoken with hundreds of caregivers. Caregivers raising underage and adult special-needs children, including those on the autism spectrum from low- to mid- to high-functioning, those with different syndromes, or one of the numerous cognitive or physical diagnoses which the CDC describes as the top forty disease states. (Great language that they use to categorize various diagnoses! Disease state! Makes me sick to my stomach).

I have also listened to hundreds more caregivers who are providing care to their spouse or life partner who has become disabled, incapacitated, diagnosed with dementia or Alzheimer's, Parkinson's or another life-altering diagnosis; caregivers caring for one or both of their aging parents, a family member with a traumatic brain injury or another life-impacting diagnosis; those caring for a family member who is a military veteran, a loved one who is sick or disabled from an accident, cancer diagnosis, loss of their ability to speak or walk or care for themselves. Caregivers across a broad spectrum of caring for loved ones in need of their time, attention, their help, compassion, and their financial resources.

Almost to a fault—though we are part of a large community (estimated to be seventy-five million caregivers in the U.S. alone)—when we are providing care to another person, it is easy to feel all alone. As if we're on some island, giving of ourselves, sometimes nonstop. And without much recognition or help from others.

To this point, I wanted to share the thoughts, feelings, and streams of consciousness of a few caregivers as they shared windows into their journey with me. What they're thinking, feeling, what's worrying them or got them all wound up. It is important to hear, in an unvarnished manner, some of their ramblings that come from their hearts. Some comments are raw, mind you. But you would expect no less because you already know some of the challenges this season brings.

Those who have chosen to share their thoughts here felt that sharing the reality of things, would help others. Maybe you will see parts of yourself in some of their streams of consciousness. Here we go.

"Romance! Are you nuts? We haven't slept in the same bed for at least three years, maybe more. Our son is nonverbal, low-functioning, on the autism spectrum. My husband, when he's home, along with the other kids and me—we're on shifts so someone is always on him at all times given he sleeps less than five hours each night. It is impossible to relax, because we never know what's coming next. We're on call 24/7, and he's only seven years old! I never expected this would be our life."
—*Mother of an underage special-needs child*

"When I look in the mirror now, I don't see me anymore. Where did I go? I used to be fun, full of energy, and up for anything. Not anymore. My husband needs me, although he no longer knows I am his wife. He'll look at me as if he knows me but doesn't know from where? He has worked his ass off for years and years. We decided to take early retirement and now this! Dementia! This came out of nowhere, like a freight train without any warning. There are days when I am so angry, I could scream. But he is my husband. What choice do I have? Until death do us part, right? He needs me, and I do my best. Friends tell me to try and be grateful for the little things! What in the hell does that mean? Grateful for what?"
—*Wife of a husband with full-on dementia*

"I'm exhausted. And I don't know when it's going to let up. Managing his medications, lifting him into his wheelchair, getting him into the car, to the bathroom, grocery shopping; anywhere! It's exhausting. And he's 195 pounds. Dealing with his episodes and his PTSD thanks to three tours in Afghanistan. We're on pins and needles around here. There's never any warning as to when he might erupt or stay in his room for days on end. Christmas dinner last year, he stayed in his room the whole time. And I'm raising two teenage boys basically all by myself, with no help! It sucks! I have had it."
—*Wife of an injured military veteran*

"You know what? I am not wealthy! And my girlfriend just told me she read some article in The Wall Street Journal which stated that an autism diagnosis is more expensive than a cancer diagnosis! Can you believe that? Maybe I'll be forced to file bankruptcy. Who the hell knows. I'm sick of battling with the insurance company on claims that should be covered. But time and again, I am forced to go toe-to-toe with these bastards to get her claims covered. And I lose most of the time. It's not fair. My daughter is thirteen, diagnosed with autism by Children's Minneapolis. I don't make a lot of money, and I worry about how I'm going to make it. It's just my daughter and me, now. Her mother left a couple years ago."

—Single father of an underage special-needs daughter

"It's like having two full-time jobs, basically. I took early retirement to care for my wife. I had to, to care for her. We have three grown children who have moved away, so they're not able to help. And even though I had to face the music and put her in an assisted living facility, which is just fifteen minutes from here, seems I am over there every day anyway, to check on her and make sure the staff is doing what they're supposed to be doing—what I'm paying for. It's almost $9,000 a month. It's not like I'm rich."

—Husband caring for his aging wife of more than forty years

"I used to be a successful female executive making serious money. But not anymore. With two children under ten, my husband suffered a traumatic brain injury from a motorcycle accident. He is relearning to walk. And maybe, he never returns to his job—don't know yet. I had to quit. There were no other options. I was sick and tired of trying to hide things from my employer. I was needing to cut out of work two to three times a week to deal with whatever. There's no way they'd allow me to stay on—no way. So, I'm home now, trying to recreate our financial life, while I raise two children and tend to my husband. I don't have a choice. Who would have ever thought? I never thought my life would look like this."

—Young wife caring for a disabled husband

"I don't feel attractive anymore. I barely get out of the house nowadays. As a single mother of a nonverbal, low-functioning, adult special-needs child with Down syndrome and managing all aspects to keep him operational, I haven't had a date in years! What's that like? I'm not into online dating. It's lonely as hell. It's just me and my son. His father couldn't handle it, so he bolted. A wild life that I lead."

—Single mother of an adult special-needs child

"My life is totally different now, it's crazy. I can't even go for a walk by myself! I have to be within earshot, just in case she begins having an epileptic seizure. And those can get nuts. She becomes combative. It is exhausting. So far, I've gotten my employer to allow me to work from home, but who knows how long they'll agree to that. It's extremely stressful and I have no help. A vacation is out of the question. I can't leave her. And I don't trust anyone else to take care of her, except me."

—*Single father of a teenage special-needs daughter*

"I really connected with this gal on Match.com. I was excited to meet her for a drink and see where things might lead. After my son's diagnosis, my wife ended up leaving the state, so I've raised him by myself for the past ten years. I made the mistake of telling this gal on Match.com that I had a special-needs son, and I was stunned by her comment. She said she appreciated me being upfront, but she didn't want to connect. She said she didn't want any added stress in her life and didn't think it made sense to meet. Can you believe that bullshit?"

—*Single father of a teenage special-needs son*

"I would like a break! One day where I could get away without anyone depending on me! A day for just me! My husband divorced me. He couldn't handle two twin special-needs boys under fifteen, both diagnosed with autism. So, he left. And our divorce was hell on wheels. I have two part-time jobs working out of the house now, so that I can care for my boys, and all that entails. Of course I love them, but I don't know how long I'll hold up doing this by myself."

—*Single mother of underage twin autistic boys*

"I'm seventy-eight years old, can't retire, and our forty-four-year-old first-born son, Andy, who has Down syndrome, lives at home with us for several reasons. Since Covid, we can't find a group home that we trust, that has the proper staffing to care for Andy. So, he's with us. It's tough. I can barely move him anymore. Thanks to Covid, he has become sedentary with his weight. I don't know what's next. It's one day at a time right now."

—*Elderly father of an adult son with Down syndrome*

"Give your life to defend our country, and then you have to fight like hell to get the care you're due from the VA? What total bullshit. Not only do I have to care for my husband who served two tours in Iraq and Afghanistan; he came home minus one leg, a hand, and major league PTSD. If that wasn't enough, I have to fight with the VA to get him the care he is due! It's not right. Give your life for your country, come home severely wounded for life—then I have to care for him and our family, while I fight with the VA? It's absolutely overwhelming! And I'm supposed to take this all in stride? What total bullshit! Caring for him has almost put me down."
—*Wife of a military veteran severely wounded from combat*

Perhaps you heard parts of yourself in these unvarnished ramblings. However, if you didn't, know that you are part of an amazing group of courageous people who are attempting to be focused on the needs of someone that they care deeply about, while denying themselves much of what's important for themselves and their own lives. This is why caregiving is challenging. It bumps up against what we want, which causes all the stress, anxiety, doubt, confusion, and anger. And that's all quite normal if we're being honest.

It also reminds us of what I shared earlier. That we enter this world needing lots of help. And that most of us will leave this world in the same fashion, needing attention and care from another person. Banding together in this phase of our lives is vital for our mental health, to power through with a sense of resiliency and compassion. Let's keep moving.

CHAPTER ONE
SPEAKING FROM EXPERIENCE—MY CAREGIVER
EXPERIENCE FROM BOTH SIDES

I mentioned earlier that I have been a sole caregiver for more than twenty years. I am the single father of an adult special-needs son diagnosed with Williams syndrome (on the autism spectrum) by Children's Hospital Minneapolis and confirmed by The University of Minnesota Hospitals. Though I cannot predict the future, he may be with me until I pass away.

Connor has rocked my world in so many ways, and he is in large part the primary inspiration behind Reach For Me, given all that has taken place in my life since his diagnosis before his third birthday. In addition to my caregiver responsibilities to my son, I have had my other foot in the world of providing care to my eighty-six-year-old mother, who passed away a short time after she was diagnosed with an inoperable stage 4 brain tumor. Therefore, it is true. Caregiving has directly impacted me and my life in immense ways—some good and some not so good. Hence, my desire to help others on this same road, which can get bumpy and cloudy.

Let me share how I came to this world of caregiving, because it certainly was not by choice.

I was the oldest of five children born into a very entrepreneurial, Catholic family, so attending church every Sunday was just as much a part of my upbringing as discussing business. After graduating college from the University of Minnesota Duluth, I started my very first business with a partner at the ripe age of twenty-six. That lead to another business, where I learned that it was fun to be self-employed though there were always surprises.

In my early thirties, I married a gal eleven years younger. She brought a three-year-old daughter to the marriage, and we began life together. Five years later, Connor was born, and life changed immediately, without any warning. We were in and out of hospitals, medical clinics, therapists, and specialists. Connor underwent test after test, as we waited for results and argued with Blue Cross Blue Shield frequently when we learned they were not going to cover various claims because they were considered experimental, which to me, was total BS. My wife and I created our own filing system to keep up with the volume of medical-oriented paperwork, doctor's reports, insurance claims, test results, etc. We also learned what an IEP (individualized education plan) was and where we could get one for Connor, which was a process in and of itself. We were assigned a case manager and pushed through the myriad hoops to jump through to advocate for our child through the county, the school system, etc.

This period was nuts, nonstop, emotional, expensive, exhausting, and stressful. The stress on our marriage was also intense. Things changed fast as we tried to figure out (with the best of doctors) what was going on with our son. At the same time, my travel schedule had to be cut back, because I needed to be there at home. So, our income dropped more than just a little bit. It was impossible to escape the stress, worry, doubts, and confusion about what our future would look like. And it was impossible to plan much of anything because of all the uncertainly around our son. The outside world had no idea about how stressful it was, nor were they willing to lend a hand. It made us feel alone. Friends stopped inviting us for dinner as they just assumed we'd say no, because of everything on our plates.

To say this period impacted everything in our lives would be a true statement.

I thought, *the next person who says to me in their puppy-dog tone, "You know what, Michael? God never gives us more than we can handle," I am going to punch in the face*! I was sick of all these outsiders offering their advice—when they did not have a special-needs child! Our life was crazy, and no one could relate. With all the uncertainty that was surrounding Connor, we'd been searching for an answer or some kind of diagnosis for almost two-and-a-half years. The stress was difficult to hide. Terrific for a self-employed entrepreneur who was supposed to be "on" for my Fortune 500 clients around the country, who were paying me serious money.

I recall my biggest general session keynote address (to date) when Microsoft Corporation hired me to speak to about six thousand attendees at their annual global convention in San Francisco. It was a big deal. I was told that Bill Gates or Steve Ballmer, the CEO at the time, would personally introduce me. They asked me to speak for two hours about the methodology that I created and trademarked (outlined in my first book), which had done very well. They wanted their people to understand how it worked and then apply it in their business building efforts.

I remember being "on" and delivering a strong keynote. However, given the stress that I was carrying, I came off the stage (to a standing ovation) and became quite emotional. The stress had consumed me. I recall Ballmer saying something like, "Get back out there and acknowledge the crowd. You did a hell of a job!"

I shared with Steve that I was very worried about my son, whom I believed was going to be diagnosed in the coming months with autism. I remember his immediate reaction: respectful. He told the security detail to take me backstage and promised that he'd take care of the crowd while I took care of myself.

This episode showed me that I was struggling big-time with the stress and anxiety that had become common in our lives. This level of intense struggle was foreign to me because I grew up as a take-charge, competitive, athletic, get-it-done kind of person.

Shortly thereafter, Connor was diagnosed with Williams syndrome and our life moved into a slow-motion movie. Years later, our marriage came unwound, we divorced (as is common among parents caring for a special-needs child), and I was thrust into an entirely new life filled with more complexity. There was no other choice available.

To say that I have changed as a result of learning how to be a caregiver over the last two decades (and counting) is an understatement. I have more compassion, understanding, and wisdom, all of which were forced on me in a trial-by-fire manner. It is impossible for any caregiver to be fully prepared for what could come at them over the course of your loved one's life. And even harder to care for someone who is not able to care for themselves.

If you'd like a more detailed account of what happened to our marriage and family during this difficult period due to the stress and added challenges, how it impacted my professional life (big-time), how the new challenges messed with my beliefs and faith life, given I knew of no one in my circle who was dealing with such intense issues, I would encourage you to get a copy of *Reach For Me: The Story of My Son Connor*, a book designed for parents and related caregivers raising underage or adult special-needs children (regardless of the diagnosis, cognitive or physical). It shares the impact of my son's diagnosis and our family's meltdown, how it impacted my career, my beliefs, and my faith life.

Parents and familial caregivers have commented that the book offers them a template that really resonates, because of how transparent I am about how caregiving upended our life and brought challenges that impacted every part of our lives (for the good and not-so-good).

However, as they say, sometimes, from the most challenging times in your life can come a new purpose or a calling, if you decide to use the experience to help many others. A few years after our divorce, I became Connor's sole legal and full-time caregiver. And over these twenty-plus years that have been about endurance and learning a new level of patience, I have been remolded and rebuilt into a more empathetic person. This season as a caregiver to my son has birthed a new mission, the result of which are these books, the processes they outline, and the related programs offered to the universe of caregivers out there through Reach For Me and our affiliates.

As I mentioned, I was also a caregiver to my mother. In her situation, her health challenges came out of left field. Her diagnosis caught us all by surprise. There were no warning signs other than a fall inside her home, leading the doctor to believe it was something with her knee. On a hunch, he ordered a full blood workup, which showed the evidence of a tumor in her brain.

She was diagnosed with an inoperable stage 4 brain tumor and given four to six months to live. She initially elected a regiment of chemo and radiation, which had little success. On day one of the treatment, she had a grand mal seizure, which almost killed her. Therefore, she chose to halt the remaining treatments. Months later, I found myself on the altar of a packed church, giving her eulogy at the mass in celebration of her life.

The responsibilities for my mother were different, and in some respects, more complex than my responsibilities for Connor's care, given the administrative work. We needed to stay on the hospice care team who was so thinly staffed and the long-term care insurance company she had purchased her policy from. This was on top of the emotional bandwidth my mom demanded. This was the result of how the tumor had taken over her personality.

We never knew what to expect when we'd visit her to attend to her needs, while riding the hospice care team and the hospital care support teams. Though both talked a fabulous game, they fell short on many occasions in terms of what they were supposed to be doing. It was exhausting micromanaging the care teams we were paying to provide care, while navigating the emotional toll that it all brings.

It was after my marriage came unwound that I was challenged (thankfully) by one of my trusted business mentors, the former president and chief executive officer of the Covey Leadership Center (Franklin-Covey), who was the architect behind the massively successful book, *The Seven Habits of Highly Effective People.*

He asked me to consider repurposing my experience and track record in building successful step-by-step programs for the corporate world which had benefited 100,000 professionals and twenty-plus Fortune 500 organizations, to building a process that would improve the lives of caregivers, by giving them the tools to build their own roadmap forward based upon their own caregiver challenges.

I am grateful for his advice and counsel. As a result, the book you hold in your hands will help you power through your caregiver journey with greater resiliency, perspective, and gratitude. Mind you, I am no psychologist, therapist, marital counselor, or a doctor. I am just a person whose life has encountered numerous twists and turns because I was called (without notice) into a world that I would never have chosen myself. My journey as a full-time caregiver has been a wild ride with numerous hills and valleys too many to mention. However, it has also provided the blessing of helping other caregivers. And this is the mission of Reach For Me: a mission that drives me and our leadership team! Caring for the caregiver.

I am grateful for the opportunity to help caregivers and families navigate the unchartered and sometimes intense waters that we find ourselves in with added strength, resiliency, perspective, and gratitude for the loved one(s) we are caring for.

Becoming a caregiver is not something any of us can plan for, in most cases. And many times, it's also not something you can see coming. This is why it is so important that we have a plan that helps us navigate all the uncharted waters to make it through and still be okay.

CHAPTER TWO
THE SCOPE OF THE CAREGIVER ISSUE

Who are the caregivers? What are we dealing with? And why does it get so intense sometimes? In the event this kind of information is important to you, our government describes the scale of the caregiver issue and its impact on our mental, emotional, physical, spiritual, and financial health. This is a brief overview to remind you of the importance of sharing our stories with one another. In the sharing, our journey ends up helping someone else navigate their own.

The Centers for Disease Control and Prevention (CDC) and the National Institutes of Health (NIH) estimate that there are thirty-five million parents or related (unpaid) caregivers who are raising an underage or an adult special-needs dependent child, and an additional forty million boomers, Gen Xers, and Gen Zers who are caring for an aging parent, spouse or life partner, military veteran, or another disabled loved one.

This means an estimated **seventy-five million** people (in our country) lead more challenging lives given the added pressures that caregiving brings. They feel the impact on them, their family, their working lives, and their financial futures. They experience, firsthand, the lack of support from friends, family, and their employer. This lack of support on many fronts feeds the anxiety most caregivers deal with. And the lion's share of us caregivers are not wealthy. We are folks who must pitch in, whether we want to or not. Most of us are simply not able to hire out the caregiver responsibilities to someone else. It's not an option for most of us.

The data suggests that caregivers have entered into one of the most emotionally and financially challenging times we have ever experienced. Arguably, the largest segment of the population struggling with mental health-oriented challenges are caregivers, because of all the stress and unknowns that lie ahead. Periods of great uncertainty, doubt, high anxiety, and depression are often the hallmarks of a caregiver's life. This can break up marriages, families, and other relationships, if not managed.

Caregiving **forces** parents and families (including extended family members like grandparents, cousins, or friends) into a whole new **season** with increased stress, anxiety, depression, and emotional and financial challenges. These hardships must be dealt with because they impact our working lives in a negative manner.

As a group, we are five to six times more likely than non-caregivers to struggle with our mental health and loss of work. Upwards of 44% of caregivers are on various medications just to cope.

Further, as a group, they are often **silent** about their caregiver responsibilities because they feel that it will hurt their employment situations or future opportunities. For the most part, they are not comfortable in opening up about their caregiver-related challenges with coworkers or with their employers. Bottom line, they don't believe their employer would empathize!

There's more data on this issue. But this information will hopefully emphasize the magnitude of how many people in our country are managing additional challenges and hardships to the best of their abilities, which I hope brings you comfort. Caregiving is a big deal for us, for our employers, for our well-being, and for that of our families. It touches all areas of our life. This information is designed to underscore the need to create your plan that can improve your life as a caregiver.

Let's keep moving.

CHAPTER THREE
CAUGHT OFF GUARD—THE CAREGIVER
PREPARATION ASSESSMENT

N one of us like being caught off guard. We like being in the driver's seat of life with our hands firmly on the wheel. **And that is precisely the problem**.

We often have no warning before the role of caregiver is thrust upon us. Being thrown into such a sudden transition can foster a laundry list of emotions, making us feel like we're all over the map and out of control.

We like everything to be in its rightful place, with our lives on track, the way **we** want them to be, so we feel good about the direction we're headed in. It gives us a feeling of confidence, which contributes to our mental health.

Then—out of nowhere, there's an interruption to our life's routine. Someone (usually close to us) needs a significant amount of our time, energy, attention, and sometimes our money! This ignites a host of emotions because it forces us to **reassess**, **reorder**, or at the very least, **rethink** our routines because someone needs us. And that is damn hard! Anyone who says otherwise is lying through their teeth!

But the bigger question is, is there anything we could do to **prepare** for this season, which often has an unknown end date? The answer is to build your plan, so you are better prepared for every potential situation.

In my own personal situation, we knew in the first year of my son's life that there were some major concerns. And that hopefully, the surgery he had at seven months old would resolve those issues, which it did not. So, the worrying continued nonstop. And we began making immediate adjustments because we had to.

But when the news was given to us from his cardiologist at Children's Hospital in Minneapolis, it was like being hit with a truckload of bricks. It felt like we were in a slow-motion movie. The finality of it all! Trying to wrap our heads around the fact that this was going to be lifelong! It was unexplainable.

In one sense, we had a two-year warning period (if you can call it that) while we searched for answers, but when our son's diagnosis was delivered to us, it changed our life immediately. I remember that day, months before

January 2001, as if it happened yesterday. It was cold out and the roads were bone-dry, as we drove down 35W on our way home after receiving the news. I was in shock. After we put Connor to bed, we got into bed and stared at the wall in silence.

And that's my point. Is it even possible to prepare yourself for life-changing news that could come at any time? My answer might seem harsh, although it's not intended to be. Significant consequences are sometimes the only thing that forces us to focus on what must be addressed and put ourselves in the second (or third) position to the person requiring our attention, care, and compassion.

Therefore, is it realistic to assume that we could be prepared for a time when we are called to change our life routines for someone else that we care about? HELL NO! It's impossible to be fully prepared.

However, is there a half-step, a thought process, or a **planning guide** that could ease us into the world of caregiving? A time that many say is one of the most challenging times in their lives because there's so much uncertainty, given you don't know how long it may last, what's coming next, or how difficult it could get. This is why it's a good idea to think about ways that could help you be better prepared.

A good place to start is to ask one important question, which is this:

What do I need to prepare for?

It's likely you won't know how long your caregiving will last, how challenging it might become, and what kinds of demands it will put on you or your family.

To help create your own Caregiver Preparation Assessment, it's wise to listen to the advice and experience of other caregivers about things that came out of left field, caught them totally off guard, or cost serious money—even things that angered them. Things that made their journey more difficult.

What is wise to prepare for will depend on who you are caring for. If you are raising an underage or adult child with special needs, your caregiving could be lifelong, like mine, even if at some point you elect some type of a group home option, if that's available to you. And even then, the caregiver responsibilities rarely subside. If you are caring for an aging parent, spouse, a military veteran, or a disabled loved one who may need round-the-clock care, there are different issues to be prepared for.

Therefore, here is a **general framework** that is customizable to your needs. It is designed to help you think through areas in your life that need attention so that you can be better prepared. Only you will know how to respond to these questions. And though you may not know the answers, you may have an instinct as to areas you should pay attention to, to protect your mental health and resiliency.

It's a framework for you and anyone else involved with you in your caregiver responsibilities. And if you are already a caregiver, this checklist can still be of great value as you go about managing your caregiving responsibilities along with all other things that are on your plate.

Remember, there is a community to support and encourage you. Take it from a person who has been a caregiver for twenty-seven years now—twenty of which have been as a single father and sole caregiver for my special-needs son.

Think about these questions and your responses to them, so you have more control of your own life on this road.

Be honest with yourself as you read through these seven areas. This is not only important stuff but critical to your mental health. What are the areas where you need to make changes in your own situation that will help you power through with more hope, more energy, a better attitude, and more resiliency? Here we go.

The Caregiver Preparation Assessment: Things to Consider

1) How Solid is Your Faith?

Now please don't WIG OUT! I am not a preacher, pastor, or priest. I was raised Catholic, am a practicing Catholic, and believe that my faith has helped carry me through some intensely challenging periods in my life, where it felt as though I was being pressed more than I could handle. It is not my place to suggest how your faith in a higher power could help you. Rather, to share that my own faith helped me power through some very difficult challenges over several years, when I was at the wall! It helped me hang on and make it through somehow. And it still does—when out-of-the-blue things happen related to my special-needs son that press all my buttons at the same time.

I know firsthand how easy it can be to fall into this "poor me" attitude, especially in times when you get no break. In these times, my faith has helped center me, which is important in maintaining good mental health and perspective when you're in the fire of caregiving that sometimes seems never-ending.

Therefore, if you are a person of faith, you can lean on your faith when your world seems upside down. For me, it has played a central role in helping make sense of all the stress, life changes, financial surprises, and the challenges thrust upon me when the clinical diagnosis of my son came at just two and a half years of age.

I remember leaning on my faith big-time to help me deal with the shock and loneliness, along with the worry about how we were going to make it through. The hard thing for me and so many other caregivers who have shared their stories is when situations arise, we are *forced* to make decisions when there is often no clear path to follow. Making decisions about the care of a loved one when you don't have a clear direction creates serious stress. This is where I learned to rely on my faith to ask for direction or some sign on which way to go. It is true. I have literally asked for direction on what to do, or which way to go. And believe me or not, it comes.

This is not a lecture or a church sermon in any way. Just brutal honesty that in some cases, I did not know which way to go, since many decisions that I had to make were in areas in which I had no experience. But my faith helped carry me through. I offer this knowing full well that this journey gets rough. And when that happens, having a belief in a higher power can provide comfort when things get crazy. Some people say that challenging times *force us* to lean not on our own understanding, but more on God. This is what I believe. And yet, to each his or her own. It is for you to decide, not me.

Different situations will present different decisions you will need to make, some of which will tug at your heart and your emotions, others on your checkbook. You'll need to figure out how to navigate given all the unknowns.

And you will rise to the occasion, which is all anyone can be expected to do.

2) How Solid is Your Relationship with Your Spouse or Life Partner?

Only you will know this, though you might not know the answer until you are in the fire. I don't much care for this overused expression, "When the going gets tough, the tough get going." However, it sets the table for how caring for another person for months or years on end tests the fabric of your relationship with your spouse or significant other. You will find out whether your relationship is as delicate or as rock-solid as you think it is.

In some respects, you don't know who you are partnered with or how they (or you, for that matter), will handle various challenges until they hit. And then, *wham!* It can be a wild ride and a real test of the relationship you are in because *everyone* has their own way of handling traumatic or highly emotional times. I don't care how long you've been married or together. When tough things are forced upon your world and it interrupts your routine, it can cause serious ripples in any relationship. For parents raising underage or adult special-needs children, research states that the divorce rates are as high as 75% or higher. This telegraphs how tough it can be on a relationship.

I remember sitting in the office of the second world famous doctor we were sent to see at the University of Minnesota Hospitals to verify Connor's clinical diagnosis, when this doctor (clearly in his eighties, who looked like a character in the movie *Back to the Future* with his white hair looking like he'd been hit by lightning) blurted, "How long have you guys been married? Hope you guys have a good marriage, because most don't make it." Wow! We were not there seeking marital advice, but we got some anyway! And it turned out to be accurate, given the strain it created on our relationship.

So again, what do you need to be prepared for? I would suggest that you guard (even protect) your marriage and relationship with your life partner as best you know how, because it **will** be tested. Be gentle. Think first before you speak. Cool it on the sharp comments. Do something out of the ordinary for them. Anything that will lighten the load and acknowledge that you know it's hard. That you are willing to move through this season committed to be there for one another, which is all you can do in uncharted waters that could last a while.

3) How Solid is Your Family Unit?

This is a mega-question. Caregiving usually involves taking care of a family member or an extended family member. Therefore, one would assume that everyone would chip in *BECAUSE* it's a member of the family. However, that's not how things roll in many families. Why? Why is it so hard (sometimes) to get everyone on the same page to meet the caregiving needs of another member of the family? There are lots of philosophies that address this and I'm not a therapist. However, I will share my opinions.

The pressures on the family unit have been increasing over the last fifteen to twenty years and they are real, putting increasing strain on the family unit. Social media's outsized influence, technology's dominance, the decline in the attendance of church (regardless of denomination), the perceived lack of value organized religion has in the eyes of the younger generations. These things (and others) intersect when the role of caregiving surfaces. Things that bump up against a person's willingness to help out, transferring the burden to **one** main caregiver in the family. And this adds to the tension in the family, once caregiving becomes necessary.

These tensions must be addressed and figured out so that you can remain a family, because caregiving can bring the family closer. I have experienced it. A deeper appreciation can be gained when the family comes together to support another who is struggling. This is the essence of the tag line for Reach For Me: *Caring for the Caregiver.*

4) How Solid is Your Working or Professional Life?

Caregiving impacts your ability to get your work done. I'll say it one more time. Caregiving can **radically impact** your ability to be productive, which impacts your ability to earn a living! And when your ability to generate money is impacted, we all get pretty damn wound up.

If you work for a company, how will they respond when you need to miss work for two to three hours once or twice a month so you can bring your mother or father (or spouse or sibling) to their doctor's appointment, which is *always* during the day! If you are self-employed, who will cover for you when you need to tend to your aging parents, spouse or life partner, or another family member? These are REAL challenges for most people, *because most of us are not wealthy,* so we must pay attention to our work. We don't have another choice. This is why caregiving can be so challenging. It cuts into our ability to work and advance our own careers. We are forced to figure out how this new "flow" is going to work.

This is one of the reasons behind the lack of trust employee caregivers have for their employers. Many view the corporate speak about how an employer understands the challenges for its employee caregivers (20% of employees) as BS. The lion's share of caregivers do not believe it is wise to share how challenging things are at home regarding their caregiving responsibilities, as they don't believe their employer would empathize. So, although the employers will claim that they want to be flexible, when the rubber meets the road, most caregivers find this not to be the case.

For those who are self-employed, like me and thousands of other small and mid-sized business owners, this is an even bigger issue. In my case, I had to come off the road (stop traveling) for an extended period (years) to raise my son, which impacted my income. All caregivers must learn to become nimbler out of necessity, juggling multiple balls in the air in order to protect our ability to earn money. Much of our anxiety is connected to our ability to keep the money coming in while we tend to our caregiving responsibilities.

5) How Solid are Your Finances?

Unless you are wealthy, which most of us are not, it is very easy to have huge anxiety about your finances, because caregiving impacts your ability to work and focus. At the same time, it costs more because we get to deal with our healthcare system! The maze of complexity, lack of transparency, the energy we have to exert to get an appointment for our loved one, and the leverage the healthcare insurance companies have over us, their policyholders, contributes to our stress level.

*This is precisely why Reach For Me has developed a **powerful toolset** that can help you combat this issue and save you thousands to tens of thousands of dollars every year by helping you resolve situations you will run into several times a year faster, for less money. You will find more information on **The Caregiver Financial Resolution Sessions** in the back of the book.*

There were many times when the medical claims related to my son's tests were not covered though we had the most comprehensive (and expensive) policy they offered. This forced me to address the claims with our healthcare insurance company, often losing those arguments and having to cover the added cost out of my own pocket. This came to tens of thousands in added expense every year for several years. Something which added to our stress. My guess is that this has happened to you as well. If so, the above sessions will teach you about a process that is effective in confronting caregiver-related matters in a way that increases the urgency and leverage around your situation and helps get issues resolved faster, for less money. Something that should make you smile.

As a caregiver, it is totally normal to get upset at the manner in which the healthcare system works (or doesn't work, depending on who you ask). Regardless of whether they are a for-profit or nonprofit organization, they are looking to make a profit. And the larger they are, the harder they are to navigate, which is by design.

Truth be told, most caregiver's finances are not that solid. The added pressures put upon us financially are very real and sometimes intense, driving up tensions in the family. This is the reason why Reach For Me is establishing **The Reach For Me Foundation**, a 501(c)(3) nonprofit designed to assist caregivers under duress who need urgent help with surprise medical-oriented expenses related to the loved one they are caring for. This falls under our mission of *Caring for the Caregiver*.

6) How Would You Rate Your Physical and Mental Health?

Most of us caregivers would like to be in better physical health. And that's the challenge. We don't have the luxury to camp out at the local health club or community center, lift weights for an hour, get on the stationary bike, sit in the sauna or hot tub to relax. Who has time for this? We know our physical health is connected to our mental health, but it is hard to carve time to address your own physical health needs. Most of us need help in this area. Sometimes, we are so exhausted that we don't feel like going to work out or even go for a walk. Instead, crashing on the couch in front of the television with a bag of chips might sound appealing.

To make it work for me, I will bring my son to the club. There are lots of eyes on him so I can work out. He bounces on the big rubber ball next to me while I ride the stationary bike. Then he brings his ball over to the weight area and continues to bounce while I do some weights. Then he will swim laps while I watch him from the sauna or hot tub. It works. However, this might not work for you. I know how crummy I feel when I don't workout. It is important because physical activity makes us healthier, helps us feel better, and improves our mental health as well. I take my son with me four to five times a week in the late afternoon. I've learned that to blow this off is not wise.

I'm not going to pressure you to buy a membership at your local community center. But if you don't have one, some kind of routine that gets you outside for a walk or a run is something you should absolutely create, even if it requires handing off your duties to someone else for a few hours.

If you don't carve time to get away, the person that ends up paying the price is **you** and the person you are caring for! No one can go for day after day, without tending to their own physical and mental health needs.

7) How Solid is Your Relationship with Your Siblings?

Another barnburner. Most of us might think our relationships with our siblings are pretty good. And then, wham! Mom or Dad needs help, a brother or sister returns from military service, or someone close to you has an accident. Immediately, your life changes. You have no idea what will be required of you or for how long. As you move into a new season of figuring things out, the uncertainty can create new tensions with siblings, which must be dealt with. Not that you need any more on your plate.

Regardless of whether you grew up in the same house, everyone has their own way of dealing with tough times. It requires reminding ourselves that just because we would handle things a certain way, does not mean our siblings will follow suit.

We are going to dive deeper into this area in the next chapter. Because sibling rivalries, sibling relationships, sibling *anything* can make caregiving more difficult than it needs to be. Unforeseen challenges between siblings arise in more than 50% of the families who are in this season. The next chapter will give you context so that you are better prepared to defuse any tensions when they arise.

In summary, these **seven** areas are offered to help you think through, assess, prepare, and protect yourself and those closest to you on your journey.

Later in the book, you will begin to build your **Personal Caregiver Roadmap** to better manage and power through. You can use these seven areas to help create your roadmap so it best serves and supports you. Your roadmap is your approach plan that you will design to assist in all areas of caregiving, so you are able to keep on keeping on while taking care of (and protecting) your own mental health, well-being, and resiliency.

CHAPTER FOUR
CONTROVERSY CENTRAL—CAN WE JUST GET ALONG?

N O ONE likes focusing on the negative. Most people feel it's a waste of a time. But you don't have to work very hard before you find a caregiver's story that involves one or two siblings, who, besides not lending a hand with the caregiving responsibilities, used the situation to bring up old family wounds or various unfinished business, further complicating the situation.

This will not be a long chapter because it doesn't need to be. I've included it as more of a heads-up. If you have siblings or half-brothers or sisters, it makes no difference what your place in the pecking order is: first child, middle child, or the baby of the family, there's research to suggest that caregiving is one of the most challenging seasons in any person's life—end of story.

And let's remember again: 95% (or more) of caregivers are not wealthy. We (as a group of people) are not typically able to hire out the caregiving to some agency. Which is why the research states that the typical caregiver spends (on average) twenty hours per week caregiving—**unpaid** of course. And those who are not caregivers wonder why we are wound like a top sometimes!

Caregivers (so says the research) are **five to six times** more likely than non-caregivers to suffer from high levels of stress, anxiety, and depression, which is serious stuff. This is why an estimated 44% of caregivers are on medications just to cope.

So, besides navigating all these new challenges in your life—which of course are in addition to the normal everyday things on your plate—you get to add one more! Dealing with all the emotional swings of a sibling or two (or your spouse or extended family member). What a treat!

Given the research around the topic of sibling infighting and family conflict that can arise, I would assume that you **will** experience this. If you end up breezing past the family disruption phase, you'll be quite lucky. However, I have to say that caregiving touches so many emotional, spiritual, and financial buttons for most of us that it is better to assume that some sensitive family-related issues will likely touch your experience.

In the next chapter, you will read about two families and the challenges they are experiencing. You will find these stories helpful as you prepare your roadmap. You will see why, shortly.

Many (maybe most) of us, from time to time, like to play armchair quarterback when we find out someone is going through tough times. In the next chapter, you will have the opportunity to play that role of therapist and counselor to the caregivers and members of the family in both stories.

You will read the stories of two different families, each dealing with caregiving-related challenges. Each family has a different background, personality, family dynamic, and set of caregiving issues they are dealing with. By peering into their lives, you can gain perspective on your own journey.

Think about how you would handle the challenges you will read about with each family. You may even find yourself in the stories. Understanding the challenges that each of these families is dealing with can lessen the conflicts within your own family.

At the end of each story, you'll be presented with questions that I urge you to answer. They are designed to foster discussion amongst you and the others providing care and support for your loved one.

Hopefully, as you discuss your responses with the others assisting you, the conversation will help ease your anxiety, and the worry that is so common among caregivers. Hopefully, this exercise produces a deeper understanding. And as you talk about the issues on your journey, these conversations can deepen relationships and help you find the courage to power through with greater resiliency, compassion, and gratitude.

More importantly, you may come to understand the blessing you have been given to learn from the loved one you are caring for. Vulnerability in others has a way of reaching into our soul, helping bring out the best in us. And isn't *that* what life is supposed to be about? Helping others who are struggling, *especially if they have been there for us in our formative years.*

Strap yourself in, as both stories will give you a window into the sometimes raw and intense reality of the caregiver-related issues these families are dealing with.

CHAPTER FIVE
THE CAREGIVER STORIES

Since I've provided the rationale of having the chance to peer into the lives of two different families, each dealing with different caregiver-related challenges, as you get closer to building your own Personal Caregiver Roadmap to address and power through the challenges you are dealing with, here we go.

Story Number One—The Gallagher Family

If there was ever the picture-perfect, model, successful Catholic family, the Gallaghers would be it. George Conrad Gallagher, with his six-foot-six frame and booming radio-quality voice, was a very successful dentist in the western suburbs of Minneapolis. He'd built a large practice over four decades and enjoyed the fruits of his success: a big home on Lake Minnetonka that looked like a replica of the White House, a new, bright white Cadillac Escalade every two years that he had washed daily, custom-made suits, crisp, white French-cuffed shirts with his initials on the left cuff, and he was a lover of fine cigars (though he knew that they stained his teeth). George always sported a tan, as if he'd just returned from his home in Mexico. He was a powerful presence in any room. Nothing was too big or too bold for George. He loved life, lived a grand lifestyle, and had story after story about his hunting trips for moose and elk all over the world.

His wife of forty-five-plus years, Shannon Marie, kept the family together. With her warm and charming presence, she was a master entertainer and an involved mother of three grown children. She had an elegance about her and was the only person able to rein George in. She managed him well, especially when he'd had too much scotch. To the outside world, they were revered as a bit of a power couple in the Twin Cities.

At mass every Sunday at 10:45 a.m. (unless it interfered with hunting), they gave heavily to the Catholic Church. So much so, that the archbishop of the archdioceses of St. Paul and Minneapolis was a close friend. He would dine at their home on the lake now and again and enjoyed the use of George's eight-seat King Air airplane from time to time for church-related business. George was generous that way.

The Gallaghers were proud parents of three very successful children.

The oldest (a bit of a snob) was Elinor Belair, named after George's mother. A six-foot-one, stocky blonde who had a talent for basketball (though not that fast), she played center on the high school team. Thanks to her team winning a state championship, she wound up with a full-ride scholarship to the University of Michigan—perhaps due to her father's close friendship with the head coach and a not-so-small donation to their athletic department. George also played at Michigan back in the day.

Elinor thought she was hot stuff and was clearly a daddy's girl. She worked it every chance she got, though she was whip smart. She graduated close to the top of her class with a double major in finance and healthcare management while playing basketball. George and Shannon rewarded her with a new white Lexus SUV upon graduation, telling her they'd cover the cost of law school at Harvard. She breezed through law school and upon graduating at the very top of her class, was snapped up by one of the largest healthcare companies headquartered in Indianapolis. She rose quickly through the ranks, becoming associate general counsel in six years, managing thirty-five in-house lawyers and seven outside law firms. She had it going on! However, she was harsh and condescending to her team (bordering on mean, according to some). She was a quick-tempered executive at a multi-billion-dollar healthcare insurance corporation, determined to climb as high as she could, steaming-rolling anyone who got in her way, while managing a truckload of litigation-related matters.

Connor Michael, the middle child and the only son, had athletic talent as well. At six foot four, he played football at Notre Dame and graduated with a degree in exercise science and kinesiology. After graduation, he accepted an assistant coaching position on the Notre Dame football staff. Although he was only a two-and-a-half-hour drive from where his sister Elinor was based, they rarely got together. He didn't much appreciate his older sister's my-way-or-the-highway style. Nor did he think much of how she'd order her husband around, who was responsible for raising their two children and managing the household. Because he didn't respect his sister, he had even less respect for her husband.

Connor had a ton of friends, was a devoted Catholic, and revered his parents. He was also a bit of a ladies' man just like his father. He was a handsome (and tan) guy in perfect shape. The Norte Dame faculty treated him like royalty, given the college was his mother's alma mater. She was a significant donor to the college.

The baby of the family, Anna Kate, was a creative type who loved to paint and do sculpture. And she loved children. After graduating from the University of Minnesota with degrees in special education and art history, she backpacked around Europe for about two years doing her art, then came back home to marry her college sweetheart, Ben. A few years later, she gave birth to twin boys who were both diagnosed at age two with severe autism, low-functioning and nonverbal. Her spirits were totally crushed. She went into a deep depression and needed medication to function and make it through. Immediately, Shannon swung into action, helping as much as she could since they lived close. George didn't know how to help, though he felt a deep sadness for Anna Kate and Ben, whom he liked even though he wasn't an athlete.

George began reading medical research to better understand the diagnosis and what it could mean for his grandsons. Without telling Anna Kate or his wife, he set up a revocable trust and began socking away money for the boys. He knew that Anna Kate would never make the kind of money she'd need to provide for her boys' anticipated medical needs. George felt proud knowing he was providing for them in the background, without any fanfare, so when Anna Kate needed to draw on those funds, they would be there. He wondered how people without financial means handled such a traumatic, lifelong diagnosis. He'd read that an autism diagnosis was more expensive than a cancer diagnosis, which scared the hell out of him.

Anna Kate's special-ed background was helpful, but she and Ben had difficulty wrapping their heads around the fact that they were going to be caregivers for as long as they were alive. Trying to digest this reality created strains on their relationship, which showed when they went to her parents' house on the lake for the family Sunday dinners. It took about an hour to get both boys ready to go. And trying to have a normal dinner conversation was impossible with two underage, low-functioning autistic boys in the house. George and Shannon took on a newfound respect for their daughter and son-in-law, watching them power through the challenges. George demanded that all medical claims not covered by insurance be given to him to take care of. And when he learned that there were several that insurance had already rejected, it pissed him off royally.

Six months prior to Christmas, one year soon after the diagnosis of his daughter's boys, George announced he was taking the family (minus the grandchildren) to Rome for Christmas. They would attend Christmas Eve mass in St. Peter's Square at the Vatican after an audience with the pope, thanks to some strings being pulled by his friend the archbishop of the archdioceses of St. Paul and Minneapolis.

The trip was amazing. But on the last day, George took a hard fall while getting off the tour bus, hitting his head on the pavement, landing him in the hospital for two days under observation. Because his vitals seemed okay, he was discharged and allowed to return home. But within a few short months, things began to change.

George always took a walk after dinner. One night he got lost and didn't return. Shannon called the police, who found him in a park about a mile from their home, agitated and confused about where he was. He had his wallet on him, so the police were able to determine where he lived and brought him home. Months later, he began forgetting the names of a few of his longest-term patients, who made comments to the front desk that George didn't seem to be himself. He was not the larger-than-life personality they had known for years.

He began coming home early, saying he wanted to rest. Something abnormal for George, who was always going a hundred miles an hour. Shannon knew something was not right, although he had been told by his primary physician one year prior that for a seventy-seven-year-old, he was as healthy as a horse.

Down to the Mayo Clinic they went for a battery of tests over two long days, along with a detailed exam by several doctors organized by his physicians in Minneapolis. The news came weeks after the tests were done. The diagnosis: early-stage dementia that they felt could progress rapidly. The doctors laid out a series of treatments that would (hopefully) delay the onset of full-on dementia, which would render him unable to work or take care of himself.

Shannon got the kids on a Zoom call one evening soon afterward to share the news, although George had no interest in being on the call. The kids took it as best they could. However, it took a while for the news to sink in that their strong and powerful father was failing. Within about twelve months, he could no longer practice dentistry. Money was never an issue for the family, thank God. But he just could not do it anymore. In time, he didn't recognize his own dental office—an office he'd had for over thirty-four years.

Day by day, Shannon, his wife of more than forty-five years, became his sole caregiver. Because of his size (six-foot-six) and her being a slight five-foot-seven, the physical work of his care became difficult. She called another Zoom meeting with the children to prepare them for how rapidly their father was declining.

Anna Kate already knew things were getting bad because she could no longer depend on her mom to help out, which forced her to quit her special-ed job at the high school so she could stay home and care for her special-needs boys. Her husband would have to find something that paid more money, so they could get along as a one-income family with two autistic underage boys. Their out-of-pocket medical costs over the last two years were upwards of $41,000. She didn't feel right about her father continuing to cover these costs.

"Hello everyone, thanks for coming together on short notice," Shannon began. *"I have some news to share and it's not good. I cannot take care of your father on my own anymore. It's been hell on wheels up here regarding how fast he is declining, and he's so damn big that I need help. I can't do it anymore by myself. It's twenty-four hours a day. He's up at all hours of the night. He tries to go down to the dock. I must have eyes on him all the time. I'm going to have a nervous breakdown. It is nuts."*

"Mother—get to the point," Elinor blurted out. *"What's the new news? We know Daddy has been in decline. So, what is the new news?"* she barked with zero emotion.

Shannon ignored her oldest daughter's harshness and continued speaking.

"Four weeks ago, your father was admitted into a high-end dementia care facility in Excelsior. Thank God they had an opening. They are outstanding. I'm over there every day to check on him and he's getting great care, even though I can tell he's pissed at me for putting him there. It's a great team caring for him but it's expensive as hell. He had a tantrum last week where he started yelling at one of the residents, so hopefully, that won't happen again, or they'll toss his butt out on the street. He's so confused. It's cruel. That's it. That's what I wanted you all to know. That your father is now in a full-time dementia care facility and is getting good care. So far, he knows who I am. But I don't know how long that will last. I have contacted a broker who deals

in selling dental practices to evaluate what it's worth. It will likely be sold. As will be the airplane. We don't need that damn thing anymore."

Anna Kate started crying as her brother Connor spoke.

"Mom—I'm driving up this weekend to be with him. I will take the week off and stay with you at the house. I need to see him. Anna Kate, will you come with me?" Connor said, holding back his tears.

"We will go together, Connor. Ben will take time off work to be with the boys," Anna said.

"Mother, I can't come at this time. I've got a massive case I need to prepare for. But do keep me in the loop about Daddy's progress. Thanks for the up-date. Gotta jump. I've got two lawyers standing at my door."

Elinor was all business. Her siblings were not surprised. She was a *taker* in their opinion, always had been.

Given the business savvy of the family, Shannon met with the family lawyers to make all the necessary changes to their will so (while George was able) he could give his wife full power of attorney on all legal documents, including changes to their will, estate plan, asset sales, etc. She felt the kids didn't need to know and didn't want to burden them with the details, though she had a good idea that things were moving much faster than she had anticipated. So much so, that she asked the archbishop if he would be willing to celebrate George's funeral mass at the cathedral in downtown St. Paul, which he agreed to, whenever that time came. Because George was larger-than-life to many, his funeral would likely draw two thousand people, maybe more.

Fast forward a few months, and his condition had worsened considerably. Shannon kept the children in the loop, though her energy level had declined because she was over at the care facility every day for at least two hours. She was exhausted and becoming a hermit of sorts in the couple's 8,500 square foot home. One day, just after she'd left him, George fell and hurt his leg badly enough that he could no longer walk to the dining room for his meals. So, they fed him in his room, which was filled with hundreds of cards from well-wishers.

It was around this time, after Shannon had been visiting him almost daily for about three months, that George no longer knew who she was. And when this sank in, she knew things were getting close. Time to reach out to the kids again. More importantly, it was time for the children to see him one last time. To be there for their father as he had been there for them. She was convinced on a recent visit that he said something like, "*the kids.*" Therefore, she knew it was time for them to see him, maybe for the last time.

Shannon began, "*Hello everyone. I'll keep this brief. Your father is asking to see you all. This may be the last time you see him. His condition is different now. I don't believe he knows who I am anymore, and there are no guarantees he'll recognize you either. That's not the point. This could be the last time we are together as a family. He's not strong enough to leave his room. They feed him in his room now. He's getting good care. He's just so very weak and can barely lift his head up. The priest has anointed him twice, but I will have him there again when we are all together. He's been given last rites by Father Flannigan. When can you all get here?*"

"*I'll leave work in the morning, Mom. Should take me nine hours to get there,*" Connor said. "*Anna Kate, can Ben cover the boys so we can go see him together?*" Anna Kate acknowledged that would work.

"*Mother,*" Elinor began, "*I know you're all going to think that I am a horrible person! But we are **all** adults here, and we all have our own way of grieving. I cannot handle seeing Daddy struggle like this, with food all over his shirt, drooling, barely able to lift his head, and likely not knowing any of us. That's **not** how **I want** to remember Daddy. I want to remember him as the strong and powerful man that he used to be. That is how I choose to remember Daddy. Therefore, I will not be coming. I am sorry. I will honor my father from where I am down here. Please keep me in the loop on how things go. Gotta jump off now. There are people here in my office regarding this lawsuit I need to prepare for. Be blessed everyone.*"

There was a long pause after Elinor signed off the Zoom call. No one said anything for like thirty seconds. They all knew she had access to the corporate jet, which could shuttle her up to Minneapolis in no time flat. Anna Kate spoke first.

"*Mother—I am sorry, but she is an absolute, narcissistic bitch! She is a to-tal bitch. I cannot believe what I just heard come out of her mouth. The lack of respect for you, Mother, as well as for Daddy, is beyond words. I can't even believe what I just heard. She is **dead** to me! There is **no excuse** for this be-havior and total lack of respect for our father. Not after everything you have both done for her, for Connor, and for me. I am sorry, but this is what Con-nor, and I have been trying to tell you about her over the years. She's all about herself, no one else! Then she ends the call telling us to BE BLESSED? What the hell. She is one sick puppy, and I want nothing to do with her! Nothing! I am sorry, but that does it for me. Connor and I will be there tomorrow night and the three of us will go over to be with Daddy. Be strong, Mother.*"

After letting what her oldest daughter said sink in, followed by Anna Kate's rant about her sister, Shannon began.

"*I don't blame you for how you feel about your older sister. Your father and I somehow failed with her, as she appears to be disconnected from reali-ty. By the end of the week, she will be written out of the will. We don't deserve the disrespect. I've had it. Your father has signed all necessary legal power of attorney rights to me months ago, so she will be out. You don't need to mention this. She'll find out soon enough. Maybe she'll file a lawsuit against the estate once she learns—who the hell knows. She is **not welcome** at your father's funeral. You can tell her that in an email after your father passes. I'm not interested in speaking with her. I've had enough of her BS over the years. Enough disrespect. Your father and I don't deserve it for all we have done. One last thing—Anna Kate, when I met with the lawyers a few months ago regarding the power of attorney stuff, they informed me that your father set up a trust for the boys to cover yours and the boys' medical needs. There's about $700,000 in that fund, and I am going to set things up so you have a monthly amount coming for you and the boys, to cover their medical needs and such. I love you both. See you tomorrow night.*"

Anna Kate sobbed when she heard this news, knowing she and the boys were going to be okay. She was lucky to have such amazing parents, though she knew that she and Ben were in for a lifelong set of challenges.

They gathered that next night around George's bed together with the priest as he administered the anointing, making the sign of the cross on his forehead. Each of the two kids and Shannon did the same. George seemed to understand what was happening. His children were there with his wife, to pay tribute and to say goodbye. It was emotional. Everyone was crying, though they all felt a genuine sense of gratitude that their father had provided an amazing life for them. He passed away later that night with his wife and **two** of his children at his bedside. A life very well lived!

Three days after George's passing, the following email was sent from Anna Kate and Connor to their oldest sister, copying the lawyer for their parents, the managing partner of a large firm in downtown Minneapolis.

Dear Elinor,

As directed by our mother, this email is to inform you that George Conrad Gallagher passed away peacefully in his sleep three days ago. His funeral will be in ten days at the basilica in downtown St. Paul celebrated by the archbishop, per the request of our mother.

Mother has instructed us to inform you that you are not welcome to attend the mass in celebration of his life. Be blessed!

Personal Regards,
Anna Kate (Gallagher) Swenson
Connor Michael Gallagher
Cc: William Shannon, Managing Partner, Best, Shannon & Flanigan, PLC

Given Elinor's "nobody tells me what to do" nature, she almost showed up at the funeral even though she was told that she was not welcome. Days before the funeral her husband filed for divorce, citing irreconcilable differences. Therefore, she was distracted and never attended. Sometimes what comes around goes around.

Caregiver Discussion Questions

While this story is fresh, I invite you to answer the questions below and discuss them with others involved in the caregiving of your loved one(s). The questions are as follows:

1) What characters did you identify with and why?
2) What characters bothered or irritated you and why?
3) Can this family pull it together? What's your advice on how to do that?
4) Do you see yourself in any characters? If so, which ones and why?
5) What lessons do you take away from this story, and how might they apply to your situation?

The power of discussing your answers with others on your caregiver journey is that these conversations can bring insights that can be helpful along your path. They can also bring healing when you share your thoughts with other caregivers because being heard brings understanding and validation.

Story Number Two—The Thompson-Keller Family

Suzanne Thompson and Kevin Keller had been married for about four years. A hard-working, middle-class couple.

Suzanne's previous marriage had ended in a bitter divorce (to put it nicely). She was awarded full legal and physical custody of their only child, a mid-functioning boy with Down syndrome, almost eleven years old now. At thirty-eight, she'd been single after the divorce for about three years and was raising her special-needs son totally on her own without any support from her ex-husband who never bonded with the boy, leaving him, the marriage, and the state. He was not involved in his son's life by his own choice. Suzanne would say that he never was.

She had a good job as director of human resources for a large Walmart just northeast of downtown Detroit. As a single mother of an almost-teenage special-needs son, she was quite lonely and struggled with depression. Because of her bouts with depression, she purchased a disability insurance policy on the suggestion of her financial planner years ago, so she had a plan if things got challenging. The plan that she bought was from a well-known insurance company that would provide a $2,000/month benefit in the event she needed to draw on it if she became disabled.

Other than work and managing two paraprofessionals and his special-education teachers so she could work, Suzanne didn't do much socializing. She wanted someone special—she was too young to be single for the rest of her life.

She'd had a horrible experience on Match a year earlier, which was still with her. She'd met someone she thought was an awesome guy, and they'd had four or five great phone conversations before they decided to meet for a drink. But right before they decided to meet up, she felt the need to be honest about the fact that she was raising a special-needs son on her own. She shared this information before they were to meet for a glass of wine. The response she got was totally unexpected.

"Hey, Suzanne," said her new friend. *"Oh my gosh. I am so sorry. You really DO have a lot on your plate. That's incredible that you are raising him totally on your own, which I am sure is challenging and stressful. I am grateful that you shared this with me ahead of time, because based upon where I am in my life, I need to be honest and say that I don't need the stress in my*

life in the event we were to get serious. I am sure this sounds terrible. But I need to be honest and say that raising an underage special-needs son with Down syndrome is a lifelong commitment and I really admire you. But I would not be up for that challenge with all the unknowns that are ahead. So, even though I was excited to meet you, I don't think it would be a good idea. I wish you the best with your son—I really do. All the best." Then he hung up.

Suzanne was so stunned that she couldn't even cry. She just lay there in bed, mulling over what he said. She couldn't believe how someone who sounded so kind would react with such callousness and not want to meet up for a harmless drink because she had a special-needs son. *Unbelievable*, she thought. Maybe she'd be single for the rest of her life. Maybe other men would view her situation the same way—like something they would not touch. She cancelled her subscription to Match the next day.

Her girlfriend had been encouraging her since that episode not to give up hope and try one more time. Eventually, she signed up again. But after about six months on Match, she was getting fed up, again. Until one day, a guy named Kevin responded, saying that he'd like to talk some evening. He said it seemed like they had some things in common and felt it might be nice to have a chat. Which they did.

Kevin was about forty-five. A proud U.S. Army veteran. He'd done three tours in Afghanistan and managed to get out of combat with both arms and both legs. However, he struggled with intense PTSD from combat missions, and, like Suzanne, was on a cocktail of anti-depressants, Zoloft, and other medications that helped him cope, even though he had his moments. He had a good job at the Chrysler factory assembling Jeeps.

He liked his job, and the medical benefits that came with the job (private insurance in addition to his VA coverage) were important because of his special-needs son, who was on the autism spectrum and in need of constant oversight.

After a short but intense (and a bit wild) courtship of less than twelve months, they married and moved into Kevin's house together; a blended family with two underage special-needs boys. One with Down syndrome, the other with autism. They knew they'd have their hands full with two special-needs boys, but the boys seemed to connect.

During their intense courtship, they both felt they should let it all hang out and share everything about their pasts to minimize any chance of divorcing a second time, which would be brutal on their sons and on their finances. The courtship was so intense that any discussion of having a pre-nuptial agreement never came up. And Susan was so attentive to Kevin's needs that he felt he'd (already) gone to Heaven.

Suzanne was fit, slight, and very much into jogging and being outdoors as much as possible. She was also structured, obsessive-compulsive, and a tad serious, with a tendency to get wrapped around the axle on a multitude of things. She also had an issue with intimacy, though she hid it very well during their courtship. But now that she was married and in a commit-ted relationship, physical intimacy was challenging because of the stress around raising her special-needs son and her job. And her son was her number one priority, which she felt she had made clear to Kevin during their courtship.

If you asked Kevin, who looked like some buff weightlifter who worked out five hours every day, physical intimacy was a top priority in his book. He thought their intense courtship was amazing. And though they both had special-needs children, they'd make time for their alone time. Kevin was assured of this.

Suzanne was deeply faith-filled, with a need to be at church on most Sundays, although she knew it wasn't Kevin's thing. The first four years of their marriage were going well for the most part. However, Kevin had begun to feel slighted over the past year in the department of intimacy. It seemed to him as though she'd turned off that switch, which he didn't appreciate. He didn't say much as he hoped that whatever was causing the decline in activity would resolve itself. However, that would not be the case.

Soon their marriage became chock-full of intense situation after intense situation, testing their resolve as a couple. Things that neither of them ever expected. Their lives as caregivers to their special-needs children were challenging enough. However, things were about to get even more chal-lenging.

Suzanne's mother, just sixty-seven years old and a vice president of hu-man resources at a hospital close by, was diagnosed with a stage 4 glioblas-toma brain tumor on the left side. She fell one night in her house, claiming that her right leg just stopped working. Suzanne's dad needed her help lifting her mother (Mary) into the car to get her to the hospital. After ex-amining her, they didn't find anything wrong with her leg, her knee, or her ankle. But the doctor ordered a full blood workup, and they found the tumor. She was given only four to six months, assuming the three-week reg-iment of chemo and radiation treatments slowed the growth of the tumor.

The news took weeks to settle in. Her mother agreed to the chemo and radiation treatments as they felt they had no choice. It was the same hospi-tal that she worked at, so the staff knew her. Being the responsible daugh-ter (and only child), Suzanne had to manage her mother's care during this time, help her father, communicate with everyone (the oncologists, her mother's primary doctors, the chemo and radiation team), and cover her son's needs, which never stopped. Her job needed attention as well or she'd be fired, though they were being pretty accommodating.

Zero time for intimacy. She simply didn't have it in her. *Kevin would need to figure this out on his own*, she thought. Of course, he would un-derstand the stress that she was under. She didn't feel any need to have a conversation about it.

The chemo and radiation almost killed her mother on the second week. She had a grand mal seizure, so they stopped the treatments and kept her in the hospital until she stabilized. Then right before they were to begin the chemo and radiation again, her mother called it off, saying, "*That's it. I'm done with this baloney. No more!*"

Her decision to stop chemo and radiation forced a transition in her care, as her mother chose to be moved to hospice with the goal of keeping her comfortable. Suzanne was distraught and began missing more time at work because of the demands. Her boss reassured her that everything was cool and other team members were covering for her.

Her boss would say, "*Family first, okay? Focus on what is most important. We've got you covered.*" Yet that would not be the case. Suzanne got called into a meeting with her boss's boss, a first-class jerk, who gave her an ul-timatum because the work was (actually) not getting done. She could re-sign, and if she agreed to sign the documents keeping things confidential, they would provide twice the severance due in addition to healthcare for six months while she searched for another opportunity. And if not, they'd have to let her go, claiming they were eliminating her position, which was absolute BS. She was stunned by their lack of civility. She took the package and never entered the store again—ever.

Unemployed, tending to her mother in hospice every day, although it was twenty-five minutes away, and tending to her special-needs son while looking for a new position, life could not get any more stressful. She told a couple of girlfriends that she felt totally abandoned by God. She felt picked on and given undue levels of stress, which she felt were unbearable.

Many of the neighbors were aware of all that was on their plates. But not one of them brought dinner over or offered to stay with the boys so she and Kevin could be with her mother. They didn't even have time to go on a walk! No help and zero acknowledgement from the neighbors who were in the know. All they offered were comments like, "*You guys are totally amazing. We don't know how you guys do it.*" Suzanne felt like throwing up when she'd hear their comments. "*Where are people when you truly need them?*" she'd say.

This echoed what her father kept saying. "*What's the matter with your goddamn neighbors? Can't they see that you guys could use a little support? I can stay with the boys, or have them come here, but I am seventy-eight years old! I can't be there every day. I know you know this, dear.*"

The hospice facility was understaffed, poorly run, and $11,000 a month. Her mother's long-term care policy didn't cover the first sixty days, based on what the policy stated. Suzanne rode the care facility staff hard to make sure her mother was getting the care she was due. Every week, she learned of some situation the staff were supposed to be handling but weren't— forcing Suzanne to get in their faces, exhausting her patience, and causing her to be short with her son and husband. She was pissed off that she had to ride the staff and the executives who owned the facility, just to get the care that her mother was due!

Overwhelmed, with no relief in sight, she did not need any more surprises as her depression was back in full swing. However, even more was ahead. Though Kevin was helping out with her mom and the boys, he'd had it in terms of the lack of intimacy—the same complaint that drove Suzanne's first husband to look elsewhere. Kevin was not up for physical intimacy a couple times a year and made that known for the first time. He told Suzanne that his friends at work had a new nickname for him: "Mr. Once-a-Semester." She didn't think that was funny. Neither did Kevin.

Within a few weeks, they were in counseling. During one session, Suzanne snapped, screaming that she had nothing more to give, and that if he couldn't stand by her, perhaps he should look elsewhere. To which he agreed. And that was that!

They began sleeping in separate bedrooms the next night, confusing the boys. They stopped speaking, except during a dinner here or there or in passing to coordinate care for the boys. One night, after she and her son had come back from visiting her mother, she came home to find a hand-written note on the kitchen counter from Kevin, saying he and his son had moved out and that he was planning to file for divorce. She grabbed her son and sobbed. *Where is God in this mess?* she thought. She called a girlfriend to come be with her. Caregiving for her son over many years, exaggerated by her mother's challenges, had frayed her ability to cope. Her dedication to her son and her mother also cost her job. But life kept moving.

The problem was, she didn't feel she could anymore. Her tank was empty!

Since neither of them had any savings, they agreed to use a mediator with the hope they could divide what they had. Her PTSD kicked in big-time during this process. Her doctors both diagnosed her with clinical depression—unable to work. They sent their reports to the disability insurance company where Suzanne had purchased her policy years earlier. A policy she'd been paying on every quarter, for almost eight years. She needed to use the monthly benefit now, and the letters from her doctors supported her claim, outlining she had clinical depression and could not work.

The insurance company rejected the claim.

They said they needed more documentation before determining the eligibility for her benefit. She flipping blew her stack! Another battle, now with a multi-billion-dollar insurance company. They had been taking her payments for eight years. But now that she needed to use the policy, they were playing games. After battling for months, with the help of one of her neighbors who was a lawyer, they finally began paying the $2,000 monthly benefit she was due. Her depression got much worse thanks to her insurance company, who saw fit to play games on a policy that clearly listed diagnosed clinical depression among the matters it was designed to cover.

The first $4,500 of her $2,000 per month benefit went to pay off the legal bill from the lawyer. She withdrew from church, from her friends, and leaned into her special-needs son for the simple peace she drew from him. She began to simplify her life after her mother passed, selling nutritional supplements out of the house.

Again, she was starting over, now as a forty-six-year-old single mother of a teenage special-needs son who depended on her. Life had become complex, and she needed to recalibrate to determine what her life should look like moving forward. Her girlfriends kept her from going dark as she searched for the right path for her and her son, as she dealt with the anger and the loneliness of being a single parent of a special-needs child.

Caregiver Discussion Questions

While this story is fresh, I invite you to answer the questions below and discuss them with others involved in the caregiving of your loved one(s). The questions are as follows:

1) What characters did you identify with and why?
2) What characters irritated you and why?
3) Can this family pull it together? What's your advice on how to do that?
4) Do you see yourself in any of the characters? If so, which ones and why?
5) What lessons do you take away from this story, how might they apply to your situation?

The power of discussing your answers with others on your caregiver journey is that these conversations can bring insights that can be helpful along your path. They can also bring healing when you share your thoughts with other caregivers because being heard brings understanding and validation.

CHAPTER SIX
THE CAREGIVER PRINCIPLES—
PURPOSE AND EVERYDAY VALUE FOR YOUR LIFE

A couple of brief analogies as we set the table together before you begin to build your roadmap forward. A roadmap that will take into account the various challenges you are dealing with and your desire to make it through.

You already know this, but it's worth bringing up now.

When people get serious about improving their physical health, they will often go on some type of exercise plan. A new regiment that forces them to behave differently. They know they must change their habits. To do that they need a **plan** that helps them stick to a new regiment. People who *really* want change in this area will invest serious money with the hope that they'll stick to their plan and accomplish their goals.

For years, I've been telling my friends that I need to focus on my physical health to get into better shape, so I have the energy to care for Connor and all that entails. Because at times, it can drain me. Yet I have one person to blame for talking a great game but not doing anything concrete to get into better shape. And that one person is me.

I know that getting into better shape will help keep my outlook more positive, since, as the sole primary caregiver for over two decades now, it can be easy for my attitude to nosedive when I'm low on energy. Therefore, having a **plan** that will help you power through all that can come at us can improve your resiliency and your outlook.

It's common sense, really. Businesses of all kinds have **plans** they attempt to follow, that help them power through the unexpected things that happen to all companies. So, as a caregiver, knowing there will be unknowns, unexpected twists and turns, and intense challenges that will come your way (if they're not already on your plate), creating your Personal Caregiver Roadmap is not only common sense—but just plain smart. You will soon see the ways in which your plan will help **protect you** and the loved one you are caring for.

Therefore, though it's early to ask these questions, I'm going to anyway, because it's important to do a self-check-in to benchmark where you are now, before you create your roadmap. Allow me to explain the rationale.

Mini Self-Check-In: Taking the Temperature of Your Engine

My son Connor and I have this expression we've been using for years now, when he gets wound up and has a hard time self-regulating his anxiety level, which happens. So, when he gets really wound up about whatever—I will say firmly, "Connor, calm your engine! Calm your engine down!" When he hears this, he knows exactly what it means and for whatever reason, he will respond positively. It's been working, because he will begin to calm himself down. Sometimes it takes a while. But he understands what it means. We will keep using it as long as it continues to work for us. *Calm your engine down*!

We all have our own engines inside. And sometimes they burn hot as a caregiver. So hot, that it can cause us to have our own meltdown, where it is easy to move into a dark place and feel as though our entire world is caving in on us. It has happened to me several times over the years. And maybe to you as well.

The point is, this self-check-in allows you to create a benchmark for yourself as to where you think you are now, versus where you are after you've built your roadmap. It's helpful because you will see your progress in the areas of emotional, physical, financial, and spiritual health. I urge you to take a few minutes to benchmark where you are now, by answering the following questions.

Mini Self-Check-In: Taking the Temperature of Your Engine

Write your answers in your book, laptop, or a notepad. No one is going to see your answers unless you share them.

Question One: How would you say you are doing right now?
___ A chocolate mess
___ About to fall apart
___ Exhausted and frayed
___ Managing things okay (so far)
___ _____ (Your own answer)

Question Two: What would help you the most right now?

___ More help/support with my caregiver responsibilities

___ More time to rest or just be alone

___ I don't know, honestly

___ Write in what you need more of right now:

_____

_____

_____

Question Three: What do you need less of right now?

_____

_____

_____

Question Four: How would you rate the temperature of your engine?

___ Very hot

___ Getting hot

___ Pretty warm

___ Okay so far

The Caregiver Principles:
Principles To Guide Your Journey and
Improve Your Life — Baseline Understanding

Primary caregivers raising and/or caring for an underage or adult special-needs child (regardless of the diagnosis), an aging parent, spouse or life partner, a military veteran, or disabled loved one have an extra life challenge. That is to care for the person you are caring for while managing all the unknowns that lie ahead for your family, marital relationship, significant other, your working life, and all other obligations.

And we start at the same basic place: the shock, confusion, sorrow, overwhelming sadness, hopelessness, or anger that can come over us when we first have a hunch that something is not right with our child, our parent, our spouse, or another loved one. Often, there is no warning that our life is about to radically change.

Then once we get the diagnosis or the formal news about whatever is ailing our child, our parent, or our loved one, we begin digesting the news and decide we are going to meet the challenges as best we can, though we have no idea what some of them might be. And this is the tough part. Facing the unknowns that could be ahead. Enough to give anyone mega-stress and anxiety, which is the norm for most of us.

The caregiver crisis (as it is referred to in the national press) is a serious issue, as documented by an ABC News piece called, "The Invisible Crisis: America's Caregiver Crisis and the $600 Billion Unpaid Cost of their Labor." It has been avoided and ignored for far too long by employers, healthcare payers, and state-based health and human services departments. I have my opinions as to why, which I'll keep to myself.

Where is the humanity in ignoring what numerous credible sources and our research institutions are calling one of the largest mental health-related issues in our country? This issue is bigger than the crisis that inspired "We Are the World." That effort addressed a few million people outside of the U.S. The caregiver crisis is inside the U.S., and it impacts an estimated seventy-five million adults! Almost 25% of our adult population.

95% of caregivers are not WEALTHY! One health insurance claim denied, one extended stay in an assisted living facility, or one sudden event can literally destroy a family! An autism diagnosis is reported to cost even more than a cancer diagnosis. I am not making this up. I am merely stating facts, which I hope, will provide you some comfort.

It is hard to view this season as a gift that you've been given. Many care-givers view it as one extremely harsh test they did not see coming. So, it's easy to feel as though we've been caught off guard. Still, from the moment we first learn that we are entering a new period in our lives that we didn't choose or have any training for, we are called to do our best for the person we are providing care for—training or no training.

Throughout this journey, we instinctively know that it will get tough at times, where we might not believe we can make it through or that we could SNAP! Keeping a calm heart is challenging. Who among us is good at being calm all the time?

The point is, we all need help to make it through the latest hardship. Anything that can help us manage all that's on our plates and still provide care for our loved ones, so we can maintain our resiliency and mental health, as we give of ourselves perhaps more than we ever have before.

This is where the Caregiver Principles can be of great help. Designed by a full-time primary (and sole) caregiver *for* caregivers, they offer a path-way to assess and take stock of the caregiver-related challenges in your own life, to address and navigate those issues to power through them with greater resiliency, perspective, and maybe even some newfound gratitude.

Caregivers who have gone before you are unified in one basic belief that caregiving is one of the most challenging **seasons** in their entire life emo-tionally, physically, financially, and spiritually. And that if you don't have a **plan** as to how you will power through this season, then GOOD LUCK!

Their coaching is that there are so many unknowns thrown your way, that if you don't have a **plan** as to how you are going to deal with this or that issue—that the added stress, anxiety, toll on your body and mind combined with the added financial pressures, can cause any person to snap or shut down.

The plan you are going to create could **save you** from snapping or bot-toming-out. Seriously. Take it from someone who has bottomed out a few times, which was not pretty. Your **plan** will help keep your head on straight.

Each one of us has a story about what it's like to be a caregiver. The emo-tional struggles of the heart, the mind, and the physical toll it takes. The anxiety around managing the unknowns and how we are going to manage financially. These issues are real to the majority of us. Your story is likely full of challenges and learnings that, if you chose to share them in your support group meetups, could help others dealing with similar circumstances. I'm not asking that you become a motivational speaker. But the sharing of your story will help other caregivers.

One final **personal disclosure** here and now, to emphasize the importance of taking this next section of material seriously. Caregiving can mess with your mental health. If you don't build your plan to navigate your path forward, it could lead to a serious mental health crisis. Here's what I mean.

A few years after Connor's formal diagnosis, my wife left the marriage, left the state, I lost my beautiful home, my career tanked, and my entire world turned totally upside down. I went from being a nationally known, sought-after thought leader and Fortune 500 keynote speaker dealing with the senior management of major corporations, to full-time caregiver of a special-needs child. I went from feeling important and accomplished, into an intense wilderness period where it seemed as though my former career was over. My self-confidence was in the basement and negative thoughts filled my mind.

Around this time, my beautiful mother volunteered to watch Connor while I went to Hawaii to (hopefully) clear my mind and think about my future. It was in Maui, on a cliff, looking out over the ocean, where a **miracle** took place.

On that cliff, during a sunset one late afternoon, I had a meltdown and called my aunt, Sister Valerie Immaculata, a Carmelite nun of forty-five-years who was the mother superior of the Carmelite Monastery in Minneapolis. I was ranting about my life, telling her that it felt as though God had a BULLSEYE on my back, and that I had no clue as to what the hell was happening with my life. Why was my beautiful life essentially being destroyed? I was so angry, I was burning up. I was screaming into the phone. Pacing back and forth on that cliff, as I tried to explain to Sister Valerie that it felt as though I was being redirected toward something else—but I had no idea what that was!

I hung on her words and followed what she told me to do. She said to go to the gift shop in the hotel, buy a yellow pad and pen, come back to that cliff, pray for God's grace, and see what comes. And I am NOT embellishing here.

About an hour or so later—sitting in that lawn chair on that cliff, a massive download came into my mind about a new direction for me and my life, along with these **principles** I am sharing with you in this book. I am **not** kidding. It all happened on that **cliff** in Hawaii. And ever since that encounter, I have never looked back. It was a miracle. It was there, when a new vision started to come into my mind.

Therefore, the building of your plan forward is very **serious** stuff. Take it that way. **Do not** allow yourself to have a mental health crisis. I don't wish it on anyone. What I learned is that caregiver stress, anxiety, and burnout are all REAL. And that the **plan** you will build by following the process laid out for you here, can literally save your life! Therefore, take this next section seriously and do the work. It can be life changing.

Analogy to the 12-Step Program from Alcoholics Anonymous (AA)

As you may be aware, the 12-step program outlined in the Big Book by the organization Alcoholics Anonymous (AA) uses this simple yet effective step-by-step program to help people who struggle with alcohol stay on track, by adhering to the roadmap outlined in the 12-step program. This approach to a real challenge for those who struggle with alcohol is responsible for saving millions of people's lives. The impact of the plan that you are about to begin is akin to the value that millions who struggle with alcohol have experienced as a game-changer in their own lives.

Your Intuition: Trust Your Instincts

We're almost ready to present the Caregiver Principles. Seven principles you will use as your guide in assessing your own caregiver situation to create your plan, which will likely give you energy, resiliency, and a new outlook to power through this period in your life. Before we begin Principle One, which is called Assess Your Situation, try this exercise to help you tap into what may be on your heart or on your mind right now!

Here's what I mean.

Many caregivers intuitively have a sense as to what needs to change in their lives to make it through. They **know** what's broken and what needs to be fixed or changed so that they can make it through. Therefore, I encourage you to do this quick exercise right here in this book. You can use it as your baseline after you have created your roadmap. I encourage you to answer the following questions with honesty.

Trusting Your Instincts Exercise: Creating Your Initial Benchmark

Question One: What needs to change in your current caregiver situation to make it through?

A) _____
B) _____
C) _____
D) _____
E) _____

Question Two: What happens if the things you've listed don't change? What are the consequences if things don't change? Be specific.

A) _____
B) _____
C) _____
D) _____
E) _____

Question Three: How will you change the things you want changed? What will you DO to change the things you want changed? Be specific.

A) _____
B) _____
C) _____
D) _____
E) _____

We will come back to your answers as you begin your roadmap forward.

Turning Inward: Opening Up and Being Honest

As you have begun to do by responding to the previous questions, as we walk through each principle to create your roadmap, your introspection and self-analysis about the issues and challenges that you feel must be addressed or resolved, know that the power comes in honestly assessing what is troubling you, sharing those things with the others on the journey with you, and coming to some form of resolution around those issues. This process will help set you free from these issues because it will give you the sense that you've done your best to address them, one by one.

The giving of yourself day after day as a caregiver is very hard at times. Those who have never done it have no idea of how taxing it can be on your mind, your emotional balance, your body, and your finances. The financial stress alone can put anyone over the edge with intense worry about how we'll punch through.

Again, those who have never been a caregiver have almost no appreciation of the fact that whatever else is going on in your life—like your job, your family needs, and your relationship with your significant other will somehow all just magically fall into place. As a sole caregiver for over twenty years now, I can tell you from lived experience that those who have never been caregivers—these folks have a hard time relating to the emotional drain, the anxiety, and the toll it takes mentally, physically, financially, and spiritually.

That needs to change if caregivers are to be more effectively supported for all the contributions they are making to their loved ones, and to society. Their sacrifices save employers and state-based health and human services (HHS) departments **billions** every year through the care they provide. This is all fact, in the event you want to do your own research into the financial value that us caregivers provide to our society.

That said, as you look inward, there will be things you are seriously bothered by related to your life as a caregiver. Some will be private. Others not so much. The issues might be between you and a spouse or life partner, your other children, extended family members, friends, an employer, etc. Remember, caregiving touches all areas.

So where does one begin to focus on the issues or situations that must be addressed, changed, or resolved for you to power through with greater strength, resiliency, a deeper faith perspective, and a more positive attitude?

The answers begin **now** as we unpack each of the seven Caregiver Principles.

CAREGIVER PRINCIPLE ONE:
ASSESS YOUR SITUATION (MAKE YOUR LIST)

It's time to get to work in the creation of your roadmap forward to improve (and protect) your own life.

To do this well, it requires you to first assess **seven** different areas of your life as a caregiver. As you know, no one can improve upon their game until they first take stock of what's going on now: what's not working, what needs to change, and what happens if things don't. This is where your self-exploration and assessment of your situation play a role in creating the roadmap you will follow into your future.

There are seven areas you will assess, which should not be difficult work by any stretch. These seven areas will lay the foundational pillars of what will be woven into your roadmap moving forward. They are as follows:

1) Mental/emotional and physical health challenges
2) Family or extended family challenges
3) Self-care-related challenges
4) Work-related challenges
5) Financial challenges
6) Faith-oriented challenges
7) Other challenges that need to be addressed

Let's take stock of these seven areas of your life as a caregiver. You may do this work in your book, a notepad, or notebook computer. I encourage you to clothe yourself in the spirit of adventure as you walk through each of the seven areas, given this work will help you create a new path forward.

As a person who has listened to hundreds of caregiver stories, I believe most caregivers already know (intuitively) what's not working for them, or what needs to change, without any prompting.

Nonetheless, for this exercise, if you need a jump-start to help think about things that are not working for you as a caregiver, below is an example of a potential response to help get your own internal juices flowing. Again, my guess is that you will already know how to answer each of these questions.

Let's begin making your list by answering the questions around each of the seven areas mentioned above.

1) **Mental/emotional and physical health challenges**

A) What's going on that's not working?
Example: I am overwhelmed with caring for my husband, who is much larger than me, physically. I am stressed, worried about doing right by him, and scared that I am making the wrong decisions. I am grieving the loss of the man I love as he slowly slips away from me.

_____

_____

B) What needs to change and why?
Example: I need help physically caring for him.

_____

_____

C) What happens if the things you've listed don't change?
Example: If I don't get help, I am afraid I will hurt him or myself and make things worse.

_____

_____

2) **Family or extended family challenges**

A) What's going on that's not working?

_____

_____

B) What needs to change and why?

_____

_____

C) What happens if the things you've listed don't change?

_____

_____

3) **Self-care-related challenges**

   A) What's going on that's not working?

   _____

   _____

   B) What needs to change and why?

   _____

   _____

   C) What happens if the things you've listed don't change?

   _____

   _____

4) **Work-related challenges**

   A) What's going on that's not working?

   _____

   _____

   B) What needs to change and why?

   _____

   _____

   C) What happens if the things you've listed don't change?

   _____

   _____

5) **Financial challenges**

   A) What's going on that's not working?

   _____

   _____

B) What needs to change and why?

_____

_____

C) What happens if the things you've listed don't change?

_____

_____

6) **Faith-oriented challenges**

A) What's going on that's not working?

_____

_____

B) What needs to change and why?

_____

_____

C) What happens if the things you've listed don't change?

_____

_____

7) **Other caregiver-related challenges that need to be addressed**

A) What's going on that's not working?

_____

_____

B) What needs to change and why?

_____

_____

C) What happens if the things you've listed don't change?

_____

_____

Congratulations! You've now assessed the caregiver-related situations or challenges you feel must be addressed or changed or resolved to power through with fewer hindrances and more resiliency. This is important self-exploration which I'd like you to consider calling your **work product**. As you build your roadmap, we will come back to your responses as you build your plan.

Thank you for taking the first step in assessing your **current situation**. You've assessed your situation and made your list! Onward to Principle Two: Release the Anger.

CAREGIVER PRINCIPLE TWO:
RELEASE THE ANGER

I f you are angry about some aspect of your life as a caregiver, welcome to the club! It is 100% NORMAL.

Here's an example of how anger can creep into our journey, magnifying the need to find a way to release it.

As I have shared, my mother was diagnosed with a stage 4 glioblastoma brain tumor and given only months to live. If that shock was not enough, the chemo and radiation regiment didn't do much, and she elected to stop the treatment and move into hospice to remain as comfortable as possible for the remaining time that she had. This all happened quickly, as us kids tried to keep up with making sure she was being attended to, while managing our own lives.

Emotions ran hot. But what made this time even worse was the constant oversight I needed to have with the hospice facility. Yes, it was well regarded in the community. And yes, it was a nonprofit. But you would have never known this based upon how they ran that facility, at a cost of about $14,850 per MONTH.

Whenever Mother was in urgent need of a nurse, all she needed to do was press this red button they put right on her lap, and one of the attendants would come within five to ten minutes. However, do you think they abided by their policies? It was more like a twenty-minute-plus response time because of how thinly staffed the place was. I was so ticked off when I learned of this.

My mom would call me crying that no one was coming to help. And I was twenty-five miles away from the facility. Talk about ANGER! I was blazing mad and demanded to meet with the head of the facility, threatening them with media coverage if they didn't shape up and deliver the kind of care that we were paying for. I've learned that this situation is more common than not across the country. It adds to our stresses as caregivers.

ANGER throughout your caregiver journey is **normal**! For God's sake, it can be a rough journey.

Here is another **personal disclosure** to set the table for this relevant principle in ALL caregiver's lives.

I grew up in a faith-based family. We were raised in the Catholic Church and went to mass almost every Sunday. My mother was a powerful force, spiritually speaking, as was my aunt Valerie, or as we were taught to address her, Mother Immaculata. She was the mother superior in charge of about forty nuns at the Carmelite Monastery an hour from our house on Lake Minnetonka.

As my mom got into her early eighties, she began sharing during our almost nightly phone calls, her spiritual beliefs about why she felt Connor was born to me, and why Reach For Me was my calling.

She would say, "Michael, you are in the refiner's fire," which is a reference from the Bible. "You are being prepared for something great. This is why Connor was given to you. You are being exposed to tremendous trials, so that you understand the challenges caregivers like you face day after day. You cannot be helpful to anyone until you have experienced all the areas of a particular situation before you can authentically help anyone else in a similar situation. You are being used to help many. Hang on! You will soon see."

She would say these things on our calls, and I would **hang** on these words because **I was so angry I could spit.**

From the shock of Connor's diagnosis (Williams syndrome on the autism spectrum) just prior to his third birthday, the next several years dealt me serious setbacks, some of which I did not know if I could punch through.

Little things, like:

1) My marriage collapsed due (in part) to the strain around caring for Connor.
2) Which forced radical changes to my work life because I was self-employed and traveling heavily,
3) Contributing to the loss of our beautiful home that I had built on five acres of land before getting married,
4) And the loss of Fortune 500 clients, who loved our program but heard I had to come off the road to care for my son, so they assumed I couldn't be available at a moment's notice. Some even broke existing contractual agreements.
5) Causing me to move into a depression while caring for Connor.
6) Forcing a reordering of everything as the sole legal guardian and full-time caregiver to my son.

I had a hard time understanding what value my faith had any more, because my challenges were constant over years. This is why she would say, "You are in the refiner's fire. Everyone has their time in the bucket."

Her coaching became more pronounced until her death weeks before her eighty-seventh birthday. Upon receiving the news of her prognosis, lying in her hospital bed, she looked up in silence as us kids stood around her bed. Then she looked at me and said, "And you will not stop Reach For Me, Michael. This is your calling. Reach For Me will rise by the grace of God!"

Not only was this an emotional time, but I was caring for two adults. Calls with her care team, oncologists, chemo and radiation teams, her hospice care team, the long-term care insurance company, calls with siblings, traveling to the hospital and hospice facilities, etc. And making sure Connor was getting what he needed, so we kept to his routine, or his world would have gone nuts. I forgot to mention that I needed to **work**! Imagine that. And the outside world wonders why we can get wound like a top sometimes.

Let's remember the motivation behind why I am sharing this laundry list of crazy things that happened in a relatively short period of time. It is not meant to come across as some cry-in-my-beer, poor me, self-directed sob story. Rather, to remind you that many of us are on a wild ride which can cause us to wonder about whether we even want to get out of bed in the morning.

Intense challenges while you are caregiving—one after the next—can cause any person to wonder what's happening with their life, moving them into a depression. That happened to me, so I know what I'm talking about. If this kind of craziness is happening in your world, please take my advice and protect your own mental health first by getting professional help, or by involving a close group of confidents around you to walk with you through the struggles. Self-isolating (which I did) is dumb. **Do not** do that. Huddle with close friends who are aware of your struggles, so they can help carry the burden, which will help you power through. Again, it is about powering through the storm.

With this disclosure as background to this important second principle called "Release the Anger," I don't care who you are, how accomplished you might be, what your place in society is, your career stature, or how strong you might be as a person. When the news hits that you have a special-needs child or your mother or father or another loved one has been diagnosed with something that might never go away—you will get **angry.**

If you disagree, it's perhaps because you're not being honest with yourself. It is news that may alter your life moving forward in ways you're not even aware of yet. Trust me. At some point, you are going to get angry.

It's a new ballgame now. A new world that you are being drawn into with a boatload of unknowns about your own life, in addition to the loved one you need to care for. It is news that could even prevent some of the dreams you've had for your own life from being realized. That's a good reason to get angry. However, you MUST learn to **release your anger**. It is essential to your mental health.

That said—is there some special formula or time-tested process that will help you release your anger? I'm not aware of one. Every caregiver must find their own way of releasing their anger, frustration, and the sorrow that can come with life-altering news about your special-needs child, your aging mother or father, a spouse, a family member who is a military veteran, or another disabled loved one.

Is it selfish to be angry when you get the news? Who cares! You have received incredibly difficult news that may take months or even years to digest. In fact, even though my son was diagnosed more than twenty-three years ago, I still find myself getting frustrated about something I can't do because of my role as a sole caregiver. Is that selfish? I guess. But I don't beat myself up about it and neither should you. Cut yourself some slack. It's hard.

Therefore, finding yourself in a frustrated state from time to time would be the norm. Another reason why caregivers need to share our stories and hear what others are dealing with. It's fuel for our souls.

Based on being the sole caregiver of my adult special-needs son for more than twenty years, I believe we caregivers will have to wrestle with this emotion called **anger** for as long as we are caregiving. We must learn how to manage it so we can be present for those we are caring for. You cannot be an effective, present caregiver for your loved one if you're all hosed up and frustrated all the time.

The only people able to comprehend how hard and lonely caregiving is, are other caregivers. They understand the loss of self. They also struggle (as do I) with not wanting to come across as a complainer. Fellow caregivers get the anger thing and the importance releasing it.

Releasing the anger will bring a new level of peace and acceptance about all the unknowns, which helps you address them one at a time, helping you become more resilient.

REFLECTION QUESTIONS FOR CAREGIVER PRINCIPLE TWO: RELEASE THE ANGER

As a part-time or full-time caregiver, there's plenty to get wound up about. How will these responsibilities impact your relationship with your significant other? How will it impact your family and extended family, in the event they don't want to lend a hand? How much will you need to be involved with the healthcare insurance and the providers? How will you navigate doctors, therapists, lawyers, assisted living facilities, dementia care facilities, county-based case managers, special-ed departments of the schools (if you are caring for a special-needs child under twenty-one), day programs, ABA therapy providers (if you have a child on the autism spectrum), Medicare and Medicaid, etc. Things that all have the capacity to make us mega-frustrated.

To help address this ever-present emotion along your caregiver journey, I encourage you to respond to the following reflection questions around this principle on your road to building your roadmap.

Reflection Questions

Question One: What are you angry about that needs to be addressed, changed, or resolved?

_____

_____

Question Two: What would others say you are angry or stressed about as a caregiver?

_____

_____

Question Three: How are you going to address or resolve them to move forward?

_____

_____

Question Four: How will you commit to do the work necessary in releasing the anger?

_____

_____

Once you write down your responses, I encourage you to talk them through with others on your journey. The goal is to reduce stress, anxiety, fear, and find some level of contentment as you move forward.

Anger, as you know, can be toxic to you, to the one you are caring for, and to everyone else around you. Therefore, getting rid of it is the goal, so we can move forward with a newfound energy and sense of purpose as a caregiver.

CAREGIVER PRINCIPLE THREE:
REQUEST/EXPECT COOPERATION

I have a good friend who is a retired Catholic priest. Someone whom I regard as a wise man, given his thirty-five-plus years serving as a highly regarded priest in the community. He used to share that as his father began to struggle, he and his siblings would have various ideas on how the family should help their father. This of course, led to some spirited conversations amongst his siblings.

He had a great line he would share whenever he was traveling to be with his father, and sometimes, with his siblings. Describing how he'd attempt to get everyone on the same page regarding caring for their father, he would say, "**We are all the same height**. We are **all** the same height."

It was a brilliant way to communicate to your siblings or your extended family involved in the caregiving, some of the following things in a rather diplomatic manner:

1) I don't care how much money you have or that you make
2) I don't care about how important you might be in your professional career
3) I don't care about your title or job function
4) I don't care about how far away you live from our father
5) I don't care about how busy you might be in your life
6) I don't care about your place in the family: oldest, youngest, middle child, etc.
7) I don't care ....

We are all the same height.

Meaning, when it comes to figuring out the issues of caring for our father, no one is any more or less important than anyone else. **We all have an equal say. We are all the same height**.

I love this analogy, because it addresses any attitude you might bump into with your siblings, ex-spouse, extended family members, or anyone that has an opinion about decisions that should be made regarding the loved one in need of care. Trust me. This is relevant to your journey.

We have already discussed in Chapter Four the various controversies and disagreements that can arise among family members when trying to make decisions that impact the person requiring the care, and how those decisions impact other family members.

As you know, just because you grew up in the same house as your siblings, does not mean you will all come together in total harmony on major decisions regarding the care of your loved one. Sure, it would be nice if that could happen, although the likelihood is less than 50% at best.

Going back to the concept of trusting your intuition, or as they say, trusting your gut, my guess is that you already know (or have a good idea) as to who in your immediate family or extended family you might lock horns with when important decisions need to be made. Listen to your instincts in this area. Maybe jot down some of the anticipated areas where potential contention or disagreement might come before you begin discussing them with other family members. This will help you to be more prepared. It will also help you remain calm during those sometimes-intense conversations.

Request and expect cooperation. Caregiver Principle Three.

It is a mindset, whether you are an only child, the oldest, youngest, or middle child. Everyone involved may have an attitude that their approach to the situation is the wisest for your loved one and everyone else. This is why taking on the mindset that you are **all the same height** is critical to arriving at decisions that are best for your loved one(s) and all others involved.

There is no need to be depressed if things become contentious because these decisions are often heavy and involve someone you care deeply about. But that is **no excuse** for not entering into these conversations with the attitude of expecting gracious cooperation from all involved.

REFLECTION QUESTIONS FOR CAREGIVER PRINCIPLE THREE: REQUEST/EXPECT COOPERATION

Family members, extended family, ex-spouses, and the like will all have an opinion on issues impacting the care of your loved one(s). Those opinions may not align with yours, which is why it is important to request and expect gracious cooperation as you discuss important decisions that need to be made.

In concert with trusting your own instincts, I encourage you to answer the following reflection questions to prepare yourself for the conversations you are bound to have going forward, if you've not already begun to have them.

Reflection Questions

Question One: What family or extended family members do you anticipate could cause issues in coming to the best approaches on behalf of your loved one(s)?

_____

_____

Question Two: What do you anticipate will be their position on important issues?

_____

_____

Question Three: How can you prepare yourself to deal with these issues in the spirit of expecting cooperation in decisions that best support your loved one(s)?

_____

_____

Once you write down your responses, I encourage you to talk them through with others on your journey. The goal is to reduce your stress, anxiety, and fear, and find a level of contentment as you move forward. Having proactive discussions around difficult decisions you need to make will foster perspective and help ward off any potentially explosive discussions, which don't serve anyone. Let's keep moving forward.

CAREGIVER PRINCIPLE FOUR:
BLOCK THE DOUBTING

IMPOSSIBE, you say! Maybe, or maybe not.

As a caregiver, doubt (especially self-doubt) can come upon us out of nowhere and have a paralyzing effect on our ability to deliver the care needed for our loved one. No self-help author, talk show personality, motivational speaker, president, king, queen, or professional athlete has any better approach on handling doubt than you or me. In fact, I would submit that we (as a group seventy-five million strong) have had more than our fair share of life interruptions. And because of this, we've been forced to deal with more intense levels of doubt, self-doubt, and fear—all of which are issues because they can paralyze us.

Doubt, like anger, can essentially ruin your life because it can strip away your energy, which you desperately need. It can also block you from experiencing those rare but tender moments with the person you are caring for. Doubt is standard course. Learning how to cope with this potentially paralyzing emotion is important so you can be at your best in your role as caregiver.

Here are two **true stories**, both of which created **doubt** for me as a caregiver. One is about my grandfather, who had Alzheimer's disease and was a handful to manage, exhausting me and our family. The other is about my (now) adult special-needs son Connor. The first story happened years ago, but I remember it as if it happened yesterday.

First the story of my grandfather.

As the oldest of five children, my father designated me as the lead caregiver to my grandfather, who was about 6 foot 4 and a former physical education teacher at a high school in the inner city. A strong, hot-tempered Irish man who loved his beer after he'd mowed the lawn, he developed dementia and then full-on Alzheimer's disease, which was intense. When he could no longer live with my grandmother, he moved into the basement of our house on the lake. Us kids (all five of us) had a shift with Grandpa during this one summer because he required twenty-four-hour supervision.

My shift was bedtime to morning. On average, he'd get up at least twice each night, put on two pair of pants and two or three shirts, and go out the door that led down to the lake and attempt to sit on the dock. It took everything to persuade him to go back to bed. I was afraid he could drown if he got into the lake. At 5 foot 11, there was no way I could handle him. After one summer of this, he had exhausted our family. My parents chose a nursing home that had an opening about twenty minutes from our house. We moved him there, as they saw no other choice to care for him.

About three times a week, I'd go see him after school to check on him (and the staff) responsible for caring for him. They were doing a so-so job on some things, and other things not at all. I'd need to trim his fingernails and toenails, as the staff never did. Irritating, since my parents were paying about $6,500 every month—thirty-five years ago. Often when I'd see him, he would swing his arms at me because he did not know who I was.

He was angry because he could not form his thoughts or recognize us kids. One time, as I was trimming his toenails, he put his foot on my chest and shoved me across the room to the wall. I hurt my back and had to miss the summer hockey captain's practices for a week. I had big doubts about whether what I was trying to do for him was working!

He was so angry that he couldn't live his life after eighty-four years, and I was worn-out. We learned that I needed someone with me so he didn't hurt me, given his size and huge frustration level, because he had no idea who I was anymore. Though I was doing my best, the disease had taken him over. His quality of life was nonexistent.

This is when I began praying that the Lord would take him. Doubt hung with our family for months as we checked on him, until we got the call one night that he had passed. They wanted me to come to verify his body before they took him. Rest in peace, Grandpa John.

The second story is about my special-needs son and how self-doubt rattled me on a particular day. It's a story about why bouts of intense doubt are common among us caregivers. And why it is important to keep humor at the ready, helping us remain lighthearted in times when we are tested beyond anything we could imagine.

Connor has several fixations he will lock onto, some of which are very intense to deal with if you're not in the right mindset. They range from an ultra-fixation on his gas-powered leaf blower and the weed whacker, to getting the mail from the mailbox (which I am NOT to go near), Halloween (candy), and his drums.

It was the summer of 2012, and Connor was almost fourteen. I'd picked him up from Club Care summer school and we were headed home as I began laying out our schedule for the evening, because he needed to understand what is coming next and in what order. Structure for Connor was and still is ultra-necessary, at his current age.

When we got home, he headed to the mailbox to check the mail. Once that box was checked, he headed straight for his gas-powered leaf blower, which provides over-the-moon satisfaction. He pulls the cord to start it, then stops it. Starts it, stops it. Starts it, stops it… etc. He calls this routine "pumping the blower." After he repeats this several times, he finally lets the damn thing run. So, there he goes in all of his glory. Shorts hanging down, mirror sunglasses on, sound deadening headphones on, rubber work gloves. He's on a mission to blow whatever is in his path: rocks, the mailbox, the shrubs, the side of the house, or the hood of my Jeep. Nothing is off limits. He's in "blower heaven" and should not be disturbed. There is zero downtime for me when he's in blower-mode. I must be watching him.

All of a sudden—I could not see him in the yard. I ran to the garage and found him standing in front of the Jeep. He had turned the blower hose on his face and was trying to cool himself down, gasoline running down his legs, sweating like a pig with dirt all over his face. I grabbed the blower, shut it off, and tried to show him the gasoline running down his leg. Let's just say that was **not** the right way to handle the situation. He slammed his headphones on the driveway, cracking them, tore off his mask, ripped off his work gloves, yelled at me, stormed into the house into his room and slammed the door so hard that the pictures on the other side of the wall came off their hooks. I had never seen him this worked up. And he could not calm himself down. He sat in his room talking to Snuffy, his blanky (who he says is from Mexico), telling Snuffy that I was a bad Daddy.

After about twenty minutes, he came out of his room, sat down, and said, "I think you are having a hard day, Daddy. I think you are confused. You took my blower. It's not right, Daddy."

Clearly, I was in the wrong. I was exhausted because it took over an hour just to calm him down. After feeding him and putting him to bed, I lay in bed numb, wondering how many more of these episodes might be ahead due to his fixations. Like his need to run his gas-powered blower every day in the summer, as I pray for snow.

These two stories are shared to help you remember the numerous caregiver stories you have endured already, some of which may have been funny and others not so much. They remind us that life is fragile, and that caring for another person is not only hard, but it presses up against much of what makes us who we are.

Moments like this require us to take a step back to assess what happened so we protect our well-being as we deliver care to another loved one and, perhaps, gain some perspective as we are delivering something called love to someone we care deeply about.

How do I block the doubting when things like this happen? I try and remind myself that it is not his fault, and that he is not trying to be mean! He is a special-needs child! He was born this way. This helps remind me to calm down and deal with the intense moments of self-doubt that still come. Maybe for you as well.

I don't believe it is realistic that you and I will get away from having to deal with self-doubt as a caregiver. However, we can manage it, just like we need to manage and release our anger from time to time.

Share your stories. They will be helpful to others in your caregiver support group meetups.

Block the doubting, Caregiver Principle Four. Something that is easy to talk about but quite another to do. It's as important as releasing the anger, so you maintain your sanity as you deliver care and compassion to your loved one.

REFLECTION QUESTIONS FOR CAREGIVER PRINCIPLE FOUR: BLOCK THE DOUBTING

As shared earlier, the answers to your reflection questions are part of your **work product** that you will use to build your roadmap. This is why your responses are important. Reflect upon the following questions regarding how this principle shows up in your life. I encourage you to discuss them with the others on this journey in addition to friends and coworkers. Just by the act of sharing your challenges, you will help others in your circle in addition to yourself.

Reflection Questions

Question One: What do you need to help cope with doubt as a caregiver?

_____

_____

_____

Question Two: How has your life changed due to your caregiver responsibilities? Honest answers only.

_____

_____

_____

Question Three: What are your biggest doubts about your future as a caregiver? Are there things you might not achieve now? What are they?

_____

_____

_____

Question Four: What are the best ways to deal with these challenges to help you power through as the best version of yourself?

_____

_____

Once you write down your responses, I encourage you to talk them through with others on your journey. The goal is to reduce your stress, anxiety, fear, doubt, and find some level of contentment as you power through.

CAREGIVER PRINCIPLE FIVE:
ACCEPT THEIR LOVE

Picture this. You're on the way to visit with your mom whom you decided (six months ago) to put into an assisted living facility with memory care services attached to it (if that became necessary) because you felt she needed to be in a safer environment. You have observed signs of dementia and think she may need those services shortly. You've not seen her for about two weeks because you were on vacation. Though your mom still recognizes you, you know it's a matter of time before she no longer does, which means it will be much harder to communicate once the disease takes over her mind. You're aware that time is short.

You're in a somber, almost pensive mood because you don't know what you're going to find when you see her this time. You're trying to be calm, though there's so much other stuff on your plate besides your mom.

You walk into her room and there she is—asleep. Hunched over in the chair. Food all over her shirt from the lunch that was served, half of which is on her tray. Her hair appears not to have been washed in days and you're wondering if she's had her sponge bath. You'll deal with the staff after your visit to find out why your mom has not had proper care, given you are paying serious money every month for her care.

As she hears you walk into her room, she wakes up, motioning to come give her a hug—food all over her shirt, and she's drooling. She wants a big hug, a kiss, and a visit about how **you** are doing. She wants to spend **time** with you. That's all. Time remembering, sharing, maybe laughing and connecting with you. That's what she wants. This was what my mom wanted every time I was with her over the last six months of her life. Time.

As the loved ones we are caring for move into the stage in their life where they become more dependent on you for their needs, a powerful thing begins to happen. They come to an (unspoken) realization that they just can't do certain things any more without help. However they come to this realization, they come to this newfound understanding that they just can't do it on their own anymore. And things such as **love** are now much more important. They want to give it and experience it.

When I was caring for my mother, even before her cancer diagnosis, she knew that things were changing. However she came to that realization, she did. And when this happened, all she wanted to do was spend **time**, remembering, sharing, and visiting. All while I was (sometimes) looking at my watch thinking about all the stuff that I had to get done. And she just wanted to give me **love**. However, I was not able to accept it sometimes because I was too busy. Shame on me. I get it now. However, she's gone now!

How nice it would be if we could accept the genuine display of love from the person we are caring for, when it doesn't necessarily come in the form or fashion or at the time that we think it should. This is another big lesson for us caregivers, because we are all confronted with this tension. Here's what I mean.

My son is cognitively challenged with his diagnosis of Williams syndrome although he is high functioning in many areas. In other areas—not so much. As he grows, he may continue to make strides in certain areas and in other areas he may not. It will be what it will be. And the experts have no clue, to be frank. But my son understands one thing very well and that is the giving of **love** unconditionally. He really doesn't understand the concept of a stranger. Nor why anyone would be disrespectful or harmful to him. In his world, everyone is a friend who should be loved.

I have watched him approach people he's never seen before with the warmest of greetings, only to watch many of them (mostly adults) not accept his warmth, but rather, attempt to understand what's different about him. And the love? It goes right by them. It was intended for them. However, they couldn't accept it. Are **you** like that?

Are you able to **accept the love** that the person you are caring for is trying to give you?

This is a mega-question to ponder because you are the only person who knows the answer. I'm not trying to bust your chops, because this is an issue all of us struggle with regardless of who we are caring for: a special-needs child, an aging parent, a spouse or life partner, an injured military veteran, or another disabled loved one.

Caregiving, as you know, can be an exhausting and draining experience because of all the energy and emotion going out of you for your loved one. And yet at the same time, consider that they, in their own way, are attempting to give you something that maybe you are not ready to receive yet. **Their love!**

One last story about my son that emphasizes this caregiver principle called "Accept Their Love."

Connor's most important holiday (still) is Halloween! Why do you suppose this is? Christmas doesn't compare. This is because candy is at the center of everything. Lucky for me, given I'm trying to watch his sugar intake. And he's crafty about how he hides muffins, candy, DOTS (which drive me nuts), etc. Like under his bed, in the drawers, his backpack, etc. In fact, weeks ago, while cleaning his sheets and remaking his bed, I found empty muffin wrappers and three empty iced tea bottles under his bed. It never stops.

A few months before Halloween, he begins his annual ritual of donning his full-blown Halloween costume, which he calls his "scary ghost mask" in front of the bathroom mirror. The ensemble includes a floor-length black cape, black gloves, and his white, scary ghost mask. He puts on his costume, mounts his bike, and rides around the neighborhood, waving with total happiness as if his costume just won "Best in Class" at the International Halloween Costume Show.

He is so happy as he rides around in his costume waving…as people are thinking, *What in the hell is that?*

Can they accept his love? Hardly. They're likely saying to themselves, *why is he doing such a crazy thing three months early*? They're not able to find the joy of such a harmless thing. Is there a lesson here?

Life is short. Yet it is so easy to get caught up in all the stress surrounding us that it is hard to acknowledge that the person we are caring for sometimes **wants to give us something**. The hope is, that we are able to accept their **love** as offered. It is there to experience from whomever you are caring for. And if you are able to accept it, you will find a new level of peace more powerful than any drug.

REFLECTION QUESTIONS FOR CAREGIVER PRINCIPLE FIVE: ACCEPT THEIR LOVE

Remember, the answers to your reflection questions are your **work product** that you will use to build your Personal Caregiver Roadmap. They are important. Reflect upon the following questions about how this principle shows up in your life as a caregiver. Then discuss them with the others on this journey, in addition to friends and coworkers. The act of sharing your challenges often ends up helping others in your circle in addition to yourself.

Reflection Questions

Question One: Are you able to accept the love from the person you are caring for?

_____

_____

_____

Question Two: If not, why? What is blocking you from accepting their love?

_____

_____

_____

Question Three: What needs to happen for you to accept their love?

_____

_____

_____

Intense questions, for sure. Which is why I encourage you to talk them through with others on the journey. The goal is to reduce your stress, anxiety, and doubt, and find a new level of **resiliency** as you power through. And the **love** and appreciation for what you are doing for someone you care deeply about.

CAREGIVER PRINCIPLE SIX:
CARVE YOUR FUTURE

Most people have a **plan for their life**. How they're going to make money, live wherever they want, get married or be single, have or adopt children, save money, buy a house or rent, protect themselves and their loved ones, travel to places they want to see, etc. Most of us have a plan. And if we're **on plan**, we feel good because we're making progress toward the kind of life that **we** want for ourselves and our family.

Then we become caregivers—and we are all of a sudden forced into looking at our plan to see if we can remain on it, or not. Or, if minor or major changes are required. It's usually dependent upon who we are caring for, the nature and the expense of the care, who will be providing that care, and a hundred other questions that will factor into your future.

And like it or not—some of your dreams may need to **change**. That alone is hard. Because caregiving could alter your future, which you didn't ask for. Yet all caregivers are faced with this real-life challenge.

The challenge of **carving your future** is often not a welcome process when you're a caregiver. Especially if things (our plan) have been on track and going pretty well. This is why this period can be a **brutal** time in any caregiver's journey. Some things may need to be reconsidered because someone close to us is faltering due to an accident, a traumatic event, or official diagnosis that forces us to take a step back. We are forced to assess this new life curveball and how it may require a reordering of certain things to keep all plates spinning at once.

For many caregivers, this is not a happy time because it can force us to change or do away with things that are very important. The changes that may be required are dependent upon who you are caring for. Here's another story from my caregiving reality as the single father and sole caregiver (that means full-time) to my adult special-needs child.

About a year after my first book published, it took off nationally and I became a national bestselling author, sought-after keynote speaker by Fortune 500 organizations, was a guest on network interviews such as CNN, CBS, ABC, NBC, Bloomberg Financial, Fox News, etc. My corporate training program based on the book was getting serious interest from companies like ADP, Microsoft, IBM, NCR, Insperity, CSC, Robert Half

International, Cap Gemini, NEC Technologies, Ceridian, and others.

I was traveling a good bit to fulfill demand for our corporate training program—then **Connor was born**! Almost overnight, things changed! Due to his challenges and the stress on our marriage, I had to cut back on travel, which meant my income dropped and for whatever reason, I had no clients in Minneapolis.

Before he was born, my professional future was clear, and everything was on track. My star was rising as a national bestselling author, Fortune 500 keynote speaker, and corporate trainer to tens of thousands of professionals in this country and abroad. And I was building a reputation as a well-respected thought leader and expert in my field.

Then came a **major** course correction, which I had **no choice** other than to accept. And when the formal diagnosis came before Christmas of 2001 from Children's Hospital Minneapolis and The University of Minnesota Hospitals, it felt as though we were under attack. One speed bump after the next, year after year.

Once we had the formal diagnosis and knew more about what we were looking at, our lives began to change around the needs of our son. There was no other option. The plans and dreams of doing certain things went out the window, and I lived for a period of years with **no clear picture** as to what the future held for me.

Close friends felt that I was in a trance. I probably was, because **my plan** had been totally derailed. My only choices were to get pissed off at the world, depressed (which happened), or I could take things day by day (for years) until I figured out our way forward based around a new life of being a full-time caregiver to my son.

The **uncertainty** we **all** have to deal with as caregivers is intense—without question. It is another reason we must protect our own mental, physical, financial, and spiritual health so that we are able to power through.

Uncertainty about our future can be dangerous, because it throws us off balance and out of our comfort zone, where we need to figure out a bunch of new things on the fly. This is often the hallmark of any caregiver's life.

This level of uncertainty can be traumatic for any caregiver who is a type-A, hard charging, get-it-done-**now** sort of person (like me); maybe you as well. No one enjoys extended periods of anxiety and uncertainty about what lies ahead for them or their loved ones. However, we caregivers live with higher levels of uncertainty about the future, because much of what's going on around us is out of our control. And **that** is what causes the anxiety, the stress, and the depression. Other times, it could cause us to surrender a bit.

Therefore, if you're saying to yourself, *No way! This guy is whacked to suggest that we carve a new future!* I get it. I really do, because I live this life every day. However, at some point, you will need to start carving your new future forward—whatever that looks like for you and your family. New pictures, dreams, plans, a different work life that better accommodates your caregiver responsibilities, etc.

I'm also encouraging you to **carve new traditions** around your life as a caregiver, whatever those might be. It won't come at once, so don't expect that it will. But after you digest and process what's going on, the learning will begin. All the adjustments that need to be made will begin. As you begin to regain some level of normalcy, if you wish to call it that, your future will begin to take shape. And when this time comes, you'll feel it and know that maybe it's time to begin carving your **new future**.

Some of us are in this caregiver world for several months. Others a few years. And some, for the rest of our lives! We all know we can't live in the past! So, what's it going to be? Carving a new plan could bring some levity, and maybe some humor to your life, which can be a lifesaver in times of intense stress.

Here's another true story to illustrate what I'm talking about regarding carving your new future.

Who ever thought that going grocery shopping at our local Target would be fun? Not me! But it can be fun. Connor has become a celebrity at our local Target. He does this dance where, after we've filled up our cart and are heading to the checkout aisle, he begins chatting up all his girlfriends at the registers. They start giving him high fives saying, "Hey, Connor! How's it going? What's going on, Connor?"

He proceeds to give them fist-pumps as if he's just hit a grand slam in the World Series. He is so proud of himself as he carries on with his pals as we go through the checkout aisle, while he puts candy into the cart that he feels we missed. Sometimes, he really works it, by grabbing some toy (usually over $100) that he feels he must have, forcing me to defuse the situation or cave in order to avoid a meltdown. This is a new tradition for us—part of carving our new future.

My career has been impacted big-time as I continue to carve my future as a sole caregiver. I have a PCA (personal caregiver attendant) now, af-ter he aged out of the school system at twenty-one years old. She is with Connor from about 9 a.m. to 3 p.m. five days each week. This window has become my new **work hours**.

My travel schedule has dropped like a rock over the years because I am the sole caregiver. My income has yet to recover from where it used to be. However, it is coming back finally. These are not easy adjustments. I have had to make the best of this new life, just as you are having to adjust and make the best of your new life.

Truth be told—you and I will likely **always** be carving our new futures based upon the adjustments we are required to make.

Therefore, regardless of whom you are caring for, we can all figure out new routines that might bring laughter or happiness to our day. This is why carving new routines is important given the stress and strain that is commonplace in our lives. Think about what that could mean for you if you embraced this principle called "Carve Your Future."

REFLECTION QUESTIONS FOR CAREGIVER PRINCIPLE SIX: CARVE YOUR FUTURE

The answers to these reflection questions are part of your **work product** you will use to build your roadmap. Reflect upon the following questions about how this principle shows up in your life. I encourage you to discuss them with others on this journey with you. The act of sharing your challenges will usually help others in your circle in addition to yourself.

Reflection Questions

Question One: What are you most fearful of not happening in your life because of your caregiver responsibilities?

_____

_____

_____

Question Two: What's the best way to address or deal with these concerns?

_____

_____

_____

Question Three: What would you really like to do in your life that you're concerned you might not be able to do because of your caregiver responsibilities?

_____

_____

_____

Question Four: List two things you could do that might bring happiness or laughter to some of your new routines as a caregiver.

_____

_____

_____

Question Five: What do you need to do to protect your sanity as a caregiver?

_____

_____

_____

These are intense questions, which is why I encourage you to talk them through with others on your journey. The goal is to reduce stress, anxiety, fear, doubt, and find a new level of contentment and resiliency as you power through. And new traditions that become part of the **new future you carve**.

CAREGIVER PRINCIPLE SEVEN:
SHARE YOUR EXPERIENCE

If you ask anyone who struggles with alcohol why they attend their weekly (or more) Alcoholics Anonymous (AA) meetings with others who struggle with the disease, you will likely get responses (as I do from my friends) like they feel a certain safety, a comfort, and automatic acceptance in sharing their challenges and struggles with alcohol with others who get it. They say the sharing of stories, challenges, and how they are dealing with them helps lighten their burden. In return, they get to listen to others dealing with many of the same challenges.

There is power, acknowledgement, and community in knowing you are not alone, but rather part of a large group of people throughout the world wrestling with the same challenges. This ritual of sharing in a group of people who have much in common, helps everyone find hope, friendship, and the strength to keep powering through.

Those who have been sober for years also like to help others make it through. It's their way of giving back because they understand the journey. And it's free. All anyone needs to do is show up to the meetings.

Much can be learned from this internationally successful model of how those struggling with alcohol come together weekly (or more), using the 12-step process outlined in the Big Book as their guide for the weekly meetups.

Reach For Me is working to put into place the same kind of weekly format (virtually or in-person) for caregivers to come together and share their stories, challenges, knowledge, and learnings in an accepting environment with other caregivers leading similar lives. There is more information at the end of the book so that you can get into a **weekly caregiver support group meetup** in your area or attend virtually. Whatever your preference.

As children, we are all taught by our parents to **share**. That it's the right thing to do. And as caregivers, my personal belief is that we've been given an opportunity to share our caregiver-related challenges, stories, and tender moments with others who are in the club. It helps us, and it helps other caregivers. Do you need any more rationale?

I'm not suggesting that you become a motivational speaker. But more than likely, there are things you've learned on your journey that will help others on theirs. Some people believe that intense hardships, challenges, or extreme difficulties sculpt the soul and the character of a person into a more complete picture of who they're designed to be. If you are one who believes in this line of thinking, I would challenge you to trust that your own caregiver experience is worth sharing with others, because your lessons learned could be of genuine benefit to them.

One word of caution, about responding when people ask you how you are doing. Ask (first) if they are a caregiver. There have been times where I've had a horrible week and have unloaded way too much information about the ups and downs to someone who is not a caregiver. And they don't know how to process that.

Remember—non-caregivers may have high regard for all that they see you do, either in church, at the grocery store, in the neighborhood, at the club, etc. By asking you how you are doing, they are showing you their regard for what you are doing. Still, you might not want to unload about all you are dealing with. They will struggle to digest it all.

REFLECTION QUESTIONS FOR CAREGIVER PRINCIPLE SEVEN: SHARE YOUR EXPERIENCE

The answers to these reflection questions are part of your **work product** you will use to build your roadmap. Reflect upon the following questions about how this principle shows up in your life. I encourage you to discuss them with others on this journey with you. The act of sharing your challenges will help others in your circle in addition to yourself.

Reflection Questions

Question One: What are the two or three things you are most proud of as a caregiver?

_____

_____

Question Two: What are the biggest things you've learned as a caregiver?

_____

_____

Question Three: How have you or your family changed because of your caregiver duties and responsibilities?

_____

_____

These are intense questions. I encourage you to talk them through with others on the journey. The goal is to reduce stress, anxiety, fear, doubt, and find a new level of resiliency to power through.

CHAPTER SEVEN
BUILD YOUR PERSONAL CAREGIVER ROADMAP FORWARD

Congratulations! I hope you are both pleased and relieved that you are in a place where you've now done much of the heavy lifting toward creating your Personal Caregiver Roadmap and a better life ahead as you move forward.

You've assessed your caregiver situation and have taken stock of what you feel needs to be addressed or changed to power through with more energy, hope, resiliency, perspective, and gratitude. AND—you have used the seven caregiver principles to guide you in reflecting on these areas that factor into the roadmap you are about to build!

This **work product** that you have now created by answering the reflection questions that were posed to you in the previous chapters is what you will now use to build your roadmap.

This should not be hard because you've done most of the work, assuming you've followed the exercises. Assuming you have—I applaud you for having the courage and the conviction to take this seriously, and to do the inner work required to assess your situation and all that is on your plate. Your dedication should pay great dividends for you as well as your family moving forward.

A couple of thoughts to take into consideration before you build your roadmap.

Like anyone who sets forth to improve their health or accomplish a task at work—those who create super-detailed plans often don't stick to their plan. They get tired looking at how involved it is. The complexity of their plan makes them discouraged and ends up working against them. Therefore, **keep yours simple.** Getting some early wins will encourage you to stay on plan and you'll feel good about the progress you are making.

Secondly, don't get wound around the axle that your plan (once you create it) is now in **cement** and that it cannot be changed. For God's sake! Who can predict what's going to happen tomorrow as a caregiver? We must remain flexible. This is **your** plan! **You can change any component at any time.** The plan must serve **you** first and then your family.

Remember the announcement that flight attendants read as they are preparing the cabin for take-off: "In the event of an unlikely loss of cabin pressure, an oxygen mask will appear from the overhead compartment. Put the mask on **yourself** first, before assisting others next to you." Your roadmap must serve **you** first because if you hit the tank and are not able to carry on, your loved one suffers even more.

It's time to build your personal caregiver roadmap. Let's finish strong toward a better life moving forward.

It's time to roll up your sleeves and create your roadmap forward to improve (and protect) your own life. Improving your mental, emotional, and financial health and resiliency, which will touch everyone.

Earlier on, in Caregiver Principle One: Assess Your Situation you assessed seven different areas of your life as a caregiver. As we said, no one can improve upon their game until they first take stock of what's going on now. You have already assessed what's not working, along with what needs to change. You've also determined what happens if things don't change.

You've done all this. You've made your list. This was your self-exploration and assessment of your current situation so you can make decisions on things that should serve you well, improving your resiliency moving forward.

Here's what we need to do next.

Review your **responses** to each of the questions you were asked around the following seven areas:

1) Mental/emotional and physical health challenges
2) Family or extended family challenges
3) Self-care-related challenges
4) Work-related challenges
5) Financial challenges
6) Faith-oriented challenges
7) Other challenges that need to be addressed

In each of the seven key areas, you were asked to respond to the following questions:
1) What's going on now that's not working?
2) What needs to change and why?
3) What happens if the things you've listed don't change?

These seven areas and your responses to the above questions (your **work product**) are what you are going to use to create your roadmap. Take your time. Go back and review your responses to all three questions for each of these **seven foundational areas** and make some decisions now as to what you want to focus on addressing, changing, or overcoming in each key area that will allow you to power through with more resiliency, perspective, and gratitude, to make your life better as you move forward as a caregiver.

As you review your responses, the goal is for you to **refine your responses and decisions into a plan** that will best help you address, or change, or overcome the key things, situations, issues, challenges, or matters that you feel need to be addressed, changed, or overcome—in order to move forward in each of the seven foundational areas.

Then you will commit those decisions that you have made into your Personal Caregiver Roadmap.

On the next several pages is the **Personal Caregiver Roadmap Template Form** for you to complete.

Don't worry about nailing it on the first pass. I've provided many pages so you can get it exactly the way you want it. If you prefer, you can build this on a yellow note pad, iPad, or your notebook computer. Whatever your pleasure.

MY PERSONAL CAREGIVER ROADMAP MOVING FORWARD

The following sets forth the key issues and challenges I am committed to address in my efforts to move forward with more resiliency, perspective, and gratitude to improve my own well-being as a caregiver, and that of my family. My important goals are as follows:

1 **Regarding my mental/emotional/physical health** challenges, I want to address/change/power though the following things:

_____

_____

_____

_____

By committing to do the following things:

_____

_____

_____

_____

2 **Regarding my family/extended family** challenges, I want to address/change/power through the following things:

_____

_____

_____

_____

By committing to do the following things:

_____

_____

_____

_____

3 **Regarding my self-care-related** challenges, I want to address/change/ power through the following things:

_____

_____

_____

_____

By committing to do the following things:

_____

_____

_____

_____

4 **Regarding my work-related** challenges, I want to address/change/ power through the following things:

_____

_____

_____

_____

By committing to do the following things:

_____

_____

_____

_____

5 **Regarding my financial** challenges, I want to address/change/power through the following things:

_____

_____

_____

_____

By committing to do the following things:

_____
_____
_____
_____

6 **Regarding my faith-oriented** challenges, I want to address/change/power through the following things:

_____
_____
_____
_____

By committing to do the following things:

_____
_____
_____
_____

7 **Regarding other caregiver-related challenges**, I want to address/change/power through the following things:

_____
_____
_____
_____

By committing to do the following things:

_____
_____
_____
_____

MY PERSONAL CAREGIVER ROADMAP MOVING FORWARD

The following sets forth the key issues and challenges I am committed to address in my efforts to move forward with more resiliency, perspective, and gratitude to improve my own well-being as a caregiver, and that of my family. My important goals are as follows:

1 **Regarding my mental/emotional/physical health** challenges, I want to address/change/power though the following things:

_____

_____

_____

_____

By committing to do the following things:

_____

_____

_____

_____

2 **Regarding my family/extended family** challenges, I want to address/change/power through the following things:

_____

_____

_____

_____

By committing to do the following things:

_____

_____

_____

_____

3 **Regarding my self-care-related** challenges, I want to address/change/ power through the following things:

_____

_____

_____

_____

By committing to do the following things:

_____

_____

_____

_____

4 **Regarding my work-related** challenges, I want to address/change/ power through the following things:

_____

_____

_____

_____

By committing to do the following things:

_____

_____

_____

_____

5 **Regarding my financial** challenges, I want to address/change/power through the following things:

_____

_____

_____

_____

By committing to do the following things:

_____

_____

_____

_____

6 **Regarding my faith-oriented** challenges, I want to address/change/
power through the following things:

_____

_____

_____

_____

By committing to do the following things:

_____

_____

_____

_____

7 **Regarding other caregiver-related challenges**, I want to address/
change/power through the following things:

_____

_____

_____

_____

By committing to do the following things:

_____

_____

_____

_____

My Personal Caregiver Roadmap Moving Forward

The following sets forth the key issues and challenges I am committed to address in my efforts to move forward with more resiliency, perspective, and gratitude to improve my own well-being as a caregiver, and that of my family. My important goals are as follows:

1 **Regarding my mental/emotional/physical health** challenges, I want to address/change/power though the following things:

_____

_____

_____

_____

By committing to do the following things:

_____

_____

_____

_____

2 **Regarding my family/extended family** challenges, I want to address/change/power through the following things:

_____

_____

_____

_____

By committing to do the following things:

_____

_____

_____

_____

3 **Regarding my self-care-related** challenges, I want to address/change/ power through the following things:

_____

_____

_____

_____

By committing to do the following things:

_____

_____

_____

_____

4 **Regarding my work-related** challenges, I want to address/change/ power through the following things:

_____

_____

_____

_____

By committing to do the following things:

_____

_____

_____

_____

5 **Regarding my financial** challenges, I want to address/change/power through the following things:

_____

_____

_____

_____

By committing to do the following things:

_____
_____
_____
_____

6 **Regarding my faith-oriented** challenges, I want to address/change/ power through the following things:

_____
_____
_____
_____

By committing to do the following things:

_____
_____
_____
_____

7 **Regarding other caregiver-related challenges**, I want to address/ change/power through the following things:

_____
_____
_____
_____

By committing to do the following things:

_____
_____
_____
_____

My Personal Caregiver Roadmap Moving Forward

The following sets forth the key issues and challenges I am committed to address in my efforts to move forward with more resiliency, perspective, and gratitude to improve my own well-being as a caregiver, and that of my family. My important goals are as follows:

1 **Regarding my mental/emotional/physical health** challenges, I want to address/change/power though the following things:

_____

_____

_____

_____

By committing to do the following things:

_____

_____

_____

_____

2 **Regarding my family/extended family** challenges, I want to address/change/power through the following things:

_____

_____

_____

_____

By committing to do the following things:

_____

_____

_____

_____

3 **Regarding my self-care-related** challenges, I want to address/change/ power through the following things:

_____
_____
_____
_____

By committing to do the following things:

_____
_____
_____
_____

4 **Regarding my work-related** challenges, I want to address/change/ power through the following things:

_____
_____
_____
_____

By committing to do the following things:

_____
_____
_____
_____

5 **Regarding my financial** challenges, I want to address/change/power through the following things:

_____
_____
_____
_____

By committing to do the following things:

_____

_____

_____

_____

6 **Regarding my faith-oriented** challenges, I want to address/change/ power through the following things:

_____

_____

_____

_____

By committing to do the following things:

_____

_____

_____

_____

7 **Regarding other caregiver-related challenges**, I want to address/ change/power through the following things:

_____

_____

_____

_____

By committing to do the following things:

_____

_____

_____

_____

Congratulations! You have just created a powerful roadmap to improve your life! A plan that should help you live with greater resiliency, perspective, and gratitude on your journey as a caregiver.

The key is staying **on plan** as you incorporate this roadmap into your life moving forward so that your own mental health and well-being is protected as you give of yourself day after day.

Where can you post your plan, so that it is in front of you every day? Living your plan should pay great dividends.

In the next chapter you will be presented with support tools to help you live your Personal Caregiver Roadmap so you see benefits in many areas of your life. Areas you decided are important enough to address, change, and power through to live your best life as a caregiver.

Thank you for your dedication to taking this material seriously. If you sincerely incorporate your new roadmap into your life, it will provide you huge dividends in so many areas of your life.

CHAPTER EIGHT
KEEPING YOUR PERSONAL CAREGIVER
ROADMAP CURRENT AND RELEVANT

Why do couples do this thing everyone calls **date night**? The answer is because it helps keep the relationship fresh, fun, exciting, and everything in between.

They do date night because it reminds them of why they chose one another, and why they made certain commitments to one another. It brings them back to what's important.

That being said—I, together with our leadership team, certified trainers, coaches, and support staff, take supporting your walk seriously. We want to help you live your best life by helping you follow your roadmap. These support tools are listed for you in the next chapter.

In a sense, you could compare the support tools to a date night. Meaning, staying connected to other caregivers on the weekly podcasts, the weekly caregiver support groups meetups (virtually or in-person), and the other tools you will learn about, will help remind you of how important it is to remain committed to living your Personal Caregiver Roadmap, so it truly helps you improve your life. It has that power, assuming you remain committed to putting your roadmap into action.

Before we share the tools that are designed to help you stay true to your roadmap, I'd like to share one last thought and story that I believe is fitting, because it touches all of us who are in this large club of millions of caregivers.

It has to do with **embracing your loved one**—regardless of how challenging it might be to care for them; a special-needs child, your aging mother or father, a spouse or significant other who is struggling, a military veteran or another disabled loved one. The thought comes from over two decades of being a full-time, sole caregiver. Therefore, please open your heart to what I am about to say.

Everyone gets surprises thrown at them over the course of their lifetime. It's unavoidable. Some of them are small and relatively easy to deal with. Others are significant, maybe causing great stress, hassle, anxiety, and uncertainty about what the future looks like. But over a relatively short period of time, you learn to deal with the setback or disappointment and move through the experience (hopefully) to a better place.

However—when you are caring for a special-needs child or an aging parent, a spouse/life partner, military veteran or another disabled family member, you often have absolutely **no idea** how long this caregiver life might last. **None.** Months, a few years, or maybe (like me), for the rest of your life. I'm not embellishing.

You often **do not know** how long you might be in this **season** of life, and neither do the medical professionals you rely on, though they'll do their best to guess. This season of uncertainty, confusion, and anxiety raises the bar on a host of emotions, some of which you never knew you had. It can eclipse you. I've seen it happen with caregivers, including myself. It can be such a life **jolt** that some simply don't recover. They can't get back on the horse of life. When this happens, it becomes a serious issue for any caregiver if not dealt with or resolved.

In these situations, a huge level of **resentment** can come out toward the person you are caring for, none of whom deserve it because (most often) it's not anyone's fault that they need your attention and care. So, instead of fostering resentment toward your special-needs child, an aging parent or relative, military veteran, or another loved one who is disabled because your world is now turned inside out, I have learned to **slow way down**.

I've cut back on or cut out activities that add to the stress of life. This (for me) has helped me to not only embrace the person that I am caring for but learn from them at the same time. I am not trying to sound like some goofball philosopher. I am being serious. I have had to slow way down to protect my mental health and well-being. This has helped me make it through on more than a few occasions.

If this sounds ridiculous to you, you may want to consider getting some professional help. It is important to get rid of any toxic resentments or anger toward life, or toward the person you are caring for. And please hear me!

Do not push them away because you are resentful of the life you are now leading as a caregiver.

It's not always going to be as challenging as it is right now. And it's not their fault in most situations. Therefore, get some professional help if you need to.

One last **story** that will bring home how flexible we must remain as caregivers, because often we don't know what's coming next.

It was the fall of 2010. A busy school day morning and for whatever reason, I was irritated about not getting various work-related things done because of the caregiver-related things for Connor. I was behind, and nothing irritates us taskmaster-type folks more than falling behind.

I dropped Connor off at school around 9:10 a.m. and headed to my office to get some writing done. However, no sooner did I get started than his school called saying that he was in the nurse's office complaining of stomach pain and wanted me to come get him.

I dropped everything, headed back up to school, picked him up, and put him in his bed to rest. About an hour later, he was crying and holding his stomach. We jumped back in the Jeep and headed straight to urgent care to see his doctor, who poked around his stomach and felt it could be his appendix.

Given it was a Friday afternoon, and the office had no CT scanning gear, they booked us into the emergency room at Children's Hospital in downtown Minneapolis. We flew downtown. We signed in and immediately prepped for a CT scan of his stomach. Sure enough, they felt his appendix had ruptured from what they could tell on the scan. Without a moment's notice, I was standing in front of the anesthesiologist listening to how they planned to put him to sleep due to his Williams syndrome diagnosis and his heart condition (aortic stenosis).

After I authorized that, the surgeon stepped forward sharing what the CT scan showed and how he felt they should proceed. These people were top-notch professionals. As I walked beside his hospital bed as they wheeled Connor into the operating room, he was clutching my hand. They slid the mask over his face, with the bubble-gum scent he picked out as they introduced the anesthesia into his system and wham—he was out. That always shakes me up. They said the procedure might take about two hours and led me to the waiting room. It was about 10:30 p.m. There I sat with my mom and a good friend worrying about whether his appendix had ruptured and what might be ahead.

The phone rang about 1 a.m. They said they got his appendix before it had ruptured, that he was in recovery, and that I could go see him in about an hour. As I entered the recovery room, there he was, already holding court with the nurses who were caring for him because he quickly learned that he could have as many popsicles as he wanted—within reason of course—which to Connor means he can have a **hundred** if he wants.

As he was chatting up both female nurses, he reached out for one of their hands, clasped it, then said to her, ever so genuinely, "I need you in my life. I just need you in my life," charming her so he could get another popsicle. "I just need you in my life!" Maybe I should try that line sometime.

As he continued to fixate on the IV that was still in his arm, as he kept telling the nurse he wanted it **out**, he leaned over to me and said, "Daddy, I think you are having a hard day. I know it's hard, but we're going to make it through."

That made me cry! My special-needs son sensed how worried I was and told me that it was going to be okay.

On this caregiver road, you and I are going to encounter things that will be **well beyond our control**, requiring lots of patience, lots of faith, and lots of emotional bandwidth to trust that we will make it through.

It is this level of uncertainty we all experience, that might help us **embrace our loved ones**. It is in the beauty of this embrace that we are reminded of the special journey we are all on.

Blessings be on you, and your loved one! Peace.

CHAPTER NINE
ONGOING CAREGIVER SUPPORT AND COMMUNITY

Together with our senior leadership team, certified trainers, caregiver coaches, and support staff, we at Reach For Me take supporting your walk seriously. We want you to live your best life by helping you follow your roadmap.

The support tools, programs, and services we offer are listed below.

1) **The Caregiver Bulletin Board:** A service allowing caregivers to connect on topics of importance, sharing information, insights, and learnings from their experiences.

2) **The Caregivers Podcast:** Weekly podcasts by RFM's founder on topics related to your roadmap, caregiver advocacy programs, and tools designed to save caregivers thousands every year, along with guests that offer information designed to improve caregivers' lives.

3) **The Caregiver Weekend Summit:** This program helps you build your Personal Caregiver Roadmap with thousands of caregivers in beautiful settings that allow you to build lasting friendships, gain insights from other caregiver's stories, and rest and reflect. It is a transformational experience.

4) **The Personal Caregiver Roadmap Digital App:** The app is designed for you to upload your roadmap, making it easy to modify anything that needs updating, helping you remain on plan.

5) **Weekly Support Group Meetups—Digital and In-Person: Weekly meetings** (virtual or in-person as local chapters are put in place) to build connections and friendships with other caregivers, share experiences and learning, helping find inspiration and resiliency to power through.

6) **Books:** *Reach For Me: The Story of My Son Connor* is an amazing story written for the thirty-five million caregivers raising underage and adult

special-needs children. It offers hope, inspiration, and techniques to power through. *The Power to Get Justice* outlines a process to address and resolve surprise medical billing and other caregiver-related matters, helping save $5,000 to $15,000 (or more) every year and resolve the issues faster. *The Caregiver Principles* is the first book in a planned series of four.

7) **Keynote Speaking:** RFM's founder has over twenty-five years of keynote speaking experience with Fortune 500 organizations such as IBM, Microsoft, ADP, CBS, Cap Gemini, Robert Half International, Insperity, NCR, Oracle and others. Given 20 percent of every employers' employees are caregivers, having an inspirational keynote as your company's kickoff to bring this program in helps honor, recognize, and pay tribute to your employee caregivers and accelerates their adoption of the program.

8) **Reach For Me Membership:** Caregivers can access the video library of material designed to help you keep moving forward in community with other caregivers.

9) **The Caregiver Resolution Program:** This program teaches caregivers how to use a proven process that helps address and resolve stressful caregiver-related matters such as surprise medical bills, insurance claims that have been denied, a matter with a school, county, provider, an assisted living/dementia care or hospice-type facility, or any number of providers that may not be providing the care that you are paying for. This program can be a lifesaver for caregivers and their families.

10) **Caregiver Program Licensing and Delivery Support:** RFM's caregiver-centric programs are designed to be licensed to employers and healthcare payers in a train-the-trainer manner so employers and payers can make them available to the 20% (or more) of their employees and policyholders who are caregivers.

For more information, please visit the website at:
www.ReachForMe.com.

CHAPTER TEN
ABOUT REACH FOR ME AND THE AUTHOR

Reach For Me's mission is to improve the lives of caregivers and their families via the caregiver-centric programs and services designed to help them build their Personal Caregiver Roadmap. This roadmap addresses all that is on their plate with the goal of helping them build a plan to help them power through with greater resiliency, perspective, and gratitude in one of the most challenging seasons of their lives.

Michael A. Boylan is the founder of Reach for Me, whose mission is to improve the lives of caregivers and families caring for underage or adult special-needs children of any diagnosis, and boomers/Gen Xers/Gen Zers caring for their aging parents, a spouse or life partner, military veteran, or disabled loved one.

He is a national bestselling author of six books and has four additional books planned. He speaks, facilitates caregiver seminars, and advises on programs the company has developed and licensed to employer organizations, healthcare plans, and state-based health and human services departments for the 20% of the citizens of each state who are caregivers. This work is improving the lives of caregivers and their families and all stakeholders directly impacted by the scope of the issue in the United States and around the world.

He is the single father of an adult son diagnosed with Williams syndrome (on the autism spectrum) whom he has raised on his own for the past twenty-plus years. He was also a primary caregiver to his aging mother. He has repurposed his professional success in corporate America to create a better life for caregivers and families based upon his lived experience.

He is a seasoned keynote speaker who has been lauded as one of the highest-rated speakers at Microsoft's Global Partners Conference where he addressed six thousand attendees about his proven step-by-step processes. Michael has appeared on CNN, ABC, NBC, CBS, Bloomberg Financial, and Fox & Friends. He lives with his special-needs son in Minneapolis and Colorado.

To contact Michael, the leadership team, learn about programs, order books, merchandise, or inquire about speaking availability, please visit www.ReachForMe.com.

Join us on weekly podcasts!

For bulk orders of the books for employers, states, and places of worship, please email: info@ReachForMe.com.

A portion of the proceeds go to The Reach For Me Foundation, a 501(C)(3) not-for-profit assisting caregivers with surprise medical bills and related issues for loved ones they are caring for and matters requiring resolution, helping caregivers save thousands every year.

For keynote speaking inquires please use the contact information below.

The Reach For Me Network, LLC
Carlson Center, 601 Carlson Parkway, Suite 1050
Minnetonka, Minnesota 55305
Office: 952-445-7854
Website: www.ReachForMe.com
General inquiries: Info@ReachForMe.com

FAITH-BASED OUTREACH—
GROWING YOUR FAITH COMMUNITY

A PILOT INITIATIVE DESIGNED TO GROW YOUR CHURCH BY MINISTER-
ING TO AN EVER-PRESENT CHALLENGE IMPACTING A SIGNIFICANT NUMBER
OF MEMBERS OF YOUR FAITH COMMUNITY

An effort designed to address and better minister to the 25% of church members who are caregivers, and another 25% of members who will be caregivers in the coming years, with material that addresses the caregiver-related challenges they are dealing with. The process will help church members improve their energy, outlook, their faith, and their resiliency to power through.

Background: Jesus was a caregiver.

He showed compassion for all those who were struggling. He understood suffering more than anyone. He comforted all those who were struggling. By his example, he has given us a model to emulate.

Due to the aging of our population in the U.S. and across the world, the topic of caregiving has become referred to as the largest mental-health-related issue in the country, according to national media and other credible sources such as the CDC and NIH. Here are some facts:

Scope of the issue for employers, healthcare payers, state-based HHS, and the church in the U.S.

1) The caregiver population is estimated at thirty-five million caring for special-needs children and forty million caring for aging parents, a spouse/life partner, military veteran, or disabled loved one. The average caregiver spends twenty hours/week (unpaid) caregiving, impacting their health.
2) 20% to 25% of all employees are caregivers. An underserved population that has entered one of the most stressful seasons in their lives.
3) Caregiving forces parents and their families into a new season with more stress, anxiety, depression, and emotional/financial hardships.
4) Caregivers are five to six times more likely to struggle with high levels of anxiety, depression, and loss of work due to caring for a loved one.

5) Upwards of 44% of caregivers are on medications due to their care-giver responsibilities to help them cope.
6) Arguably, the largest segment of the population struggling with mental health-oriented challenges are caregivers.
7) The ABC News piece, "America's Caregiver Crisis; The $600 Billion in Unpaid Cost of their Labor" shares the scale of the issue.
8) Of the congregants in any church, 25% are caregivers now; another 25% will be caregivers shortly; another 25% require care.

The Caring for the Caregiver Pilot Initiative with Participating Churches

(Becoming Stronger as a Church by Addressing the Real-World Challenges of Caregivers)

In large measure, employer organizations, the healthcare system and state-based HHS departments have ignored the issue. This creates an opening for the church to demonstrate leadership, by bringing to the caregiver population in your faith community a caregiver-centric program (via a book that outlines the step-by-step process, the Caregiver Weekend Summit Seminars delivered in larger venues, and the PCR digital app) to what the CDC estimates are seventy-five million caregivers in the U.S.—44% of whom are on medications just to cope.

The process is called the Personal Caregiver Roadmap. It allows caregivers and families to assess and better navigate the various challenges on their plate and create their roadmap for how they will power through with greater energy, faith, resiliency, and outlook during one of the most challenging seasons in their lives. The roadmap then fosters the weekly caregiver meetups in the church.

As *The Purpose Driven Life* book drove Purpose Driven Life Weekly Study Groups in thousands of churches across the country, this material fosters **weekly caregiver meetups** in your church, facilitated by the lay caregivers trained to facilitate the weekly caregiver meetups in your church.

The meetups allow caregivers to find community, friendship, support, and inspiration from others dealing with the same challenges, helping them power through and also grow in their faith walk. Pilots of the program are tailored in collaboration with church leadership.

Because most people turn to their church community *first* for support, this initiative allows the church to pilot the material, the weekly meetups, and monthly support provided lay facilitators running the meetups.

An outreach designed to grow your faith community.

For additional information please reach out to us at:
info@ReachForMe.com.

Personal Notes